BILATERAL STUDIES
IN PRIVATE INTERNATIONAL LAW

ARTHUR NUSSBAUM, Editor

NINA MOORE GALSTON, Assistant Editor

No. 1
AMERICAN-SWISS
PRIVATE INTERNATIONAL LAW
Second Edition

by
ARTHUR NUSSBAUM

Published for the

PARKER SCHOOL OF FOREIGN AND COMPARATIVE LAW
COLUMBIA UNIVERSITY IN THE CITY OF NEW YORK
WILLIS L. M. REESE, Director

by
OCEANA PUBLICATIONS, NEW YORK
1958

PREFACE

In the Introduction to the first edition of this study, the following program was submitted:

> The "Bilateral Studies" in private international law are designed to supplement the traditional methods followed in the literature and teaching of this field. The traditional approach is "universal," and rightly so; even where the textbook or essay is based on the Conflicts law of a single country, say of the United States or of France, relations of that country to the whole world abroad are contemplated. The bilateral studies will be devoted exclusively to relations between two specified countries. The special investigation required for this purpose will often disclose much relevant material overlooked or neglected in general studies. The resulting advantage to the practitioner is obvious. But in many cases it will also be possible to contribute to the general theory of private international law by way of bilateral research.
>
> For the purpose of the planned series it is not necessary to take the term "private international law" in any technical sense. All legal relations affecting the position of the individual in the international sphere may be made subjects of the intended inquiry, including, e.g., taxation and the right to work. Procedural matters, such as jurisdiction of courts, enforcement of foreign judgments, and proof of foreign law, should likewise form an important part of "bilateral" studies.

I had first offered a program of this kind in the *Columbia Law Review* of March 1947, along with an inquiry into the American-Swiss situation. The program was in part inspired by the belief that the conflict of laws doctrine in this country had concentrated too much on the entanglements of the American *state* laws. But the main motive was the conviction that the traditional private international law doctrine was too much dominated by a speculative devotion to the "law of nations." I felt that systematic analyses of the particular conflict-of-laws problems existing between two definite countries might offer a helpful supplementation—that such works would indicate a more realistic approach, involving a kind of "fact research." The tremendous difficulties of such an undertaking are obvious, but thanks to the vigorous support of the Parker School and to the cooperation of many scholars, American and foreign, the program could be realized. Eight pertinent studies have been published so far, and considerably more are being prepared.

The first edition of the study on American-Swiss Private International Law is out of print. Moreover, the problems involved have increased and broadened since its publication, and it also seemed desirable to indicate something more about the political and economic factors. Hence the contents of the study had to be rearranged to a large extent.

Regarding the American aspects of the Study, the author feels deeply indebted to Mrs. Nina M. Galston for her splendid and indefatigable cooperation. Sincere thanks are also expressed to Dr. W. Schaumann, lecturer of international law at the University of Zürich, and to Mr. Jacques Guyet, advocate in Geneva, for many helpful suggestions.

August 1958   ARTHUR NUSSBAUM

Table of Contents

ABBREVIATIONS

United States

The standard abbreviations have been used. For the convenience of non-American readers, some explanations may be given here. Federal court decisions refer to the official reports. U.S. = reports of the Supreme Court of the United States. T.C. = reports of the Tax Court. Fed. or F.2d = reports of the other federal courts. Cir. = Court of Appeals. E.D., N.D., S.D., W.D., = Eastern District, Northern District, etc.

Decisions of state courts are cited from the official as well as from the (unofficial) National Reporter System, if the case has been reported in both. For instance, 109 Misc. 696, 181 N.Y. Supp. 336 (Surr. Ct. 1919) means (N.Y.) Miscellaneous Reports (official), N.Y. Supplement (unofficial) and Surrogate's Court. N.Y.L.J. = New York Law Journal, used where no other source is available.

"Stat." means Statutes at Large, the official collection of United States laws. TS = Treaty Series, TIAS = Treaties and Other International Acts Series, UST = United States Treaties and Other International Agreements and EAS = Executive Agreement Series.

Switzerland

AS=Amtliche Sammlung der Bundesgesetze und Verordnungen der Schweizerischen Eidgenossenschaft (after 1948, Sammlung der eidgenössischen Gesetze)

BGE=Amtliche Sammlung der Bundesgerichtsentscheide

B1ZR=Blätter für Zürcherische Rechtsprechung

BS=Bereinigte Sammlung der Bundesgesetze und Verordnungen 1848-1947

NAG=Bundesgesetz vom 25. Juni betreffend die Zivilrechtlichen Verhältnisse der Niedergelassenen und Aufenthalter

OR=Bundesgesetz vom 30. März betreffend die Ergänzung des Zivilgesetzbuches (Fünfter Teil) (Obligationenrecht)

Rep=Repertorio Giurisprudenza Patria

SchwJbIntR=Schweizerisches Jahrbuch für internationales Recht

Semjud=Semaine judiciaire

SJZ=Schweizerische Juristen-Zeitung

ZBJV=Zeitschrift des Bernischen Juristenvereins

ZGB = Schweizerisches Zivilgesetzbuch vom 10. Dezember 1907

ZSR = Zeitschrift für Schweizerisches Recht

Chapter I

MATTERS OF SUBSTANTIVE LAW

A. Background

The Convention of Friendship, Reciprocal Establishments, Commerce and for the Surrender of Fugitive Criminals of November 25, 1850[1] was the starting point of private international relations between the United States and Switzerland. This was the first major agreement between the two republics[2] and the first general convention concluded by Switzerland. It was followed by the establishment of permanent diplomatic representation.

The motives behind the convention were political as well as commercial. In 1848 Switzerland had adopted a democratic and federative constitution on the American model,[3] defying the hostile attitude of the autocratic governments of Austria, France, Prussia and Russia,[4] and the government of the United States wanted to give moral support to the democratic cause. As President Furrer of the Swiss Confederation put it in a message to the Swiss Federal Assembly, President Taylor of the United States wished to extend to Switzerland "a fraternal hand in the very midst of the storms with which she was threatened, and to offer her a treaty of friendship whereby the two freest peoples on earth will treat each other reciprocally on a footing of equality."[5] A most-favored-nation clause which was embodied in articles VIII through XII of the treaty set up a barrier against the

---

[1] 11 Stat. 587; 2 W. M. Malloy, *Treaties, Conventions, International Acts, Protocols and Agreements Between the United States of America and Other Powers* 1776-1909 (1910), 1763; AS V, 201; BS 11, 773. The various documents regarding the negotiation of the treaty are fully reproduced in 5 H. Miller, *Treaties and Other International Acts of the United States of America* (1937), 845 ff. The provisions still in force are reprinted *infra* Appendix I.

[2] It was preceded only by the American-Swiss Treaty Regarding the Disposal of Property and the Succession Thereto of May 18, 1847, 9 Stat. 902; 2 Malloy, *op. cit. supra* note 1, at 1762; 5 Miller, *op. cit. supra* note 1, at 169.

[3] Replaced by the Constitution of May 29, 1874, AS I, 1; BS 1, 3.

[4] 5 Miller, *op. cit. supra* note 1, at 859.

[5] *Id.* at 865. The American special agent who conducted the negotiations, Mr. Ambrose Dudley Mann, also mentioned that, by virtue of the treaty, "our countrymen who shall visit the Old World may find a home in its centre where they will be as well protected in their persons and their property as if they were residing in their own native land." *Id.* at 862.

engulfment of Switzerland in the German *Zollverein* or any other
exclusive economic system. No wonder that the autocratic powers
tried to obstruct ratification of the treaty by representations made
to the Swiss government, particularly with reference to article I, in
"a dictatorial rather than a persuasive tone."[6] These attempts were
unsuccessful, but ratification of the treaty was long delayed due to
differences arising mainly from state and cantonal difficulties, and
leading to a few minor amendments. Ratifications were finally exchanged on November 8, 1855.

Articles VIII through XII of the treaty, which dealt with tariff provisions based on the most-favored-nation clause, were terminated in
1900 at Swiss insistence because of an unsatisfactory interpretation of
the clause by the United States.[7] Not until January 9, 1936 were
they replaced by a Reciprocal Trade Agreement,[8] which has since
undergone several changes.[9] Articles XIII through XVII of the treaty,
concerned with extradition, were superseded and expressly repealed
by the Extradition Treaty of May 14, 1900;[10] supplementary conventions were entered into on January 10, 1935 and January 31, 1940.[11]

In addition to these modifying agreements, some new bilateral
treaties have been concluded between the two countries, especially
on taxation.[12] Both countries have also joined a few multipartite conventions, particularly on copyrights and patents.[13] Yet the Treaty of
1850, apart from its historical significance, remains the most important arrangement between the two countries from the standpoint of
private international law, at least when this term is taken in the broad
sense indicated in the Program of these Studies.[14]

The tremendous rise of the United States, the favorable conditions it offers to immigrants, and its democratic spirit, have proved
very attractive to the Swiss people.[15] Sometimes, after living in the
United States, Swiss citizens have returned to their homeland, leav-

---

[6] *Id.* at 883.

[7] Notice of termination was given by the United States on March 23, 1899,
effective March 23, 1900. See 5 Miller, *op. cit. supra* note 1, at 902-903.

[8] 49 Stat. 3917; EAS 90; 171 LNTS 231; AS 52, 242; BS 14, 653.

[9] Agreement of October 13, 1950, TIAS 2188; 2 UST 453; 133 UNTS 33;
AS 1951(I), 74 (escape clause).
Agreement of June 8, 1955, TIAS 3328; 6 UST 2845; AS 1955, 561.

[10] 31 Stat. 1928; TS 354; AS 18, 633; BS 12, 267.

[11] 49 Stat. 3192; TS 889; 159 LNTS 243; AS 51, 406; BS 12, 269.
55 Stat. 1140; TS 969; AS 57, 398; BS 12, 268.

[12] *Infra* pages 43-46.

[13] *Infra* pages 41-43.

[14] *Supra* page 3.

[15] Swiss immigration into the United States from 1820 to 1956 amounted to
316,250. *Statistical Abstract of the United States* (1957), 94.

ing property in this country; others have included Swiss relatives in their American wills. Hence questions of inheritance are of particular importance in American-Swiss private international law.[16] Dual citizenship presents another important problem.[17]

Yet the situation is changing to some extent. Through the industry of her people and the evolution of technique, Switzerland has largely overcome the difficulties created by her geographic situation. Foreign capital has been attracted by the strict neutrality which has saved Switzerland from war for a century and a half and by favorable domestic legislation. The strength and stability of the Swiss franc are symptomatic, and have led to the complete elimination of exchange control in American-Swiss monetary relations.[18] A less favorable aspect of Swiss neutrality appears in the reverse situation — namely, where investments in the United States, though nominally Swiss, are actually controlled by interests deemed hostile by the American government.[19]

The democratic approach has also assumed slightly different aspects in the two countries, and this may lead to a different approach to the solution of concrete problems. While American democracy has developed certain features which might be termed socialistic, Swiss democracy is far more conservative. American anti-trust laws and the elaborate control of stock exchanges and banking,[20] as opposed to Swiss *laissez-faire* and strict laws of bank secrecy, are cases in point. Another striking, and in a sense symbolic, contrast is provided in the monetary field. While in the United States private persons are not permitted to keep gold coins, Switzerland has admitted free gold trade and even issued gold coins (the first called "*vreneli*," with a gold content of 20 francs),[21] thereby providing a chance to hoard against unfavorable national developments.

These differences, however, should not be overrated. There definitely still exists a good feeling between the two countries, although this writer believes that in Switzerland that feeling is more perceptible among workers than among members of the upper class, which is still largely influenced by a centuries-old aristocracy.

B. *International Bill of Rights*

The first article of the Treaty of 1850 contains what may be termed an international bill of rights such as is usually found in treaties of

---

16 *Infra* pages 23-32.
17 *Infra* pages 16-20.
18 A few restrictions existed between 1943 and 1950. H. Frey, *Die Devisengesetzgebung der Schweiz* (loose-leaf, 1946-[1958]), ch. 9.
19 *Infra* pages 36-37.
20 *Infra* page 38.
21 *Cf.* Amonn, "Sind Sovereigns and Vreneli Geld?", ZBJV 92, 345 (1956).

commerce.[22] According to that article, the citizens of both countries "shall be admitted and treated upon a footing of reciprocal equality in the two countries." This concession is elaborated by the text of the article in various ways. All treaty aliens "shall be at liberty to come, go, sojourn temporarily, domiciliate or establish themselves permanently"; they may "manage their affairs"(!), "exercise their profession, their industry, and their commerce"; they may "consign their products and their merchandise, and * * * sell them by wholesale or retail" either on their own or through brokers or agents, and so on. The value of this verbose explanation is greatly reduced, however, by a reservation stating that the admission and treatment granted "shall not conflict with the constitutional or legal provisions" of the contracting parties, *including those of the states and cantons.* One-sided restrictions, old and new, were thus broadly sanctioned. This fundamental qualification is re-emphasized by the clause stating that the treaty aliens concerned and the members of their families are "subject to the constitutional and legal provisions aforesaid" and that the "liberties" are conceded to those "yielding obedience to the laws, regulations, and usages of the country." Only "pecuniary or other more burdensome" conditions must not be imposed on the admitted persons, unless those conditions are also imposed on the country's own citizens.

A further limitation was sought by the United States during World War I. The government required the registration, as enemy aliens, of foreigners born in Germany or Austria; this decree affected, among others, German- and Austrian-born women who had become Swiss citizens by marriage. While the American government relied on the treaty reservation of "legal provisions", the Swiss government pointed out that this did not justify such discrimination among citizens of a neutral nation, a point which would seem to be well taken under the general law of neutrality.[23] No similar registration was decreed by the United States in World War II.

However, one will agree with the Supreme Court of the United States, which held in *Patsone* v. *Pennsylvania*[24] that the treaty right of a Swiss citizen to "carry on trade" did not prevent the State of Pennsylvania from interdicting the possession of shotguns and rifles by aliens.

---

[22] See, *e.g.*, H. C. Hawkins, *Commercial Treaties and Agreements* (1951), 14.

[23] 4 W. Burckhardt, *Schweizerisches Bundesrecht* (1931), §1862. The Swiss protests were raised in 1918 and 1919.

[24] 232 U.S. 138 (1914). Patsone was an Italian citizen, but the American-Swiss treaty was in point because of a most-favored-nation clause in the American-Italian treaty of 1894, which permitted Patsone to rely on the American-Swiss convention.

On the Swiss side, Bern authorities in 1922 denied an American citizen permanent sojourn or establishment in the canton.[25] This was allegedly on the basis of cantonal law, but there is no explanation.

A little more is known about a case which occurred in 1924, when American Mormon missionaries were denied extension of cantonal residence because of disturbances they had caused in Swiss families. The American envoy raised objections, apparently in the belief that the Swiss government intended to exclude the Mormons from Switzerland solely because of their faith, but he did not pursue the protest after he was informed of the facts.[26]

The first and decisive step rendering effective article I of the treaty is admission into the country. In the United States such admission is granted upon fulfillment of the legislative requirements. In Switzerland it is simply an administrative affair.

Originally the United States permitted free immigration, and it was only after World War I that quantitative legislative restrictions were introduced.[27] In 1921 as a rule of emergency, and in 1924 as a definite legislative action, the number of immigrants was limited by the establishment of quotas for the various countries involved. Thereafter restrictions became increasingly stringent, culminating in the provisions of the so-called Immigration and Nationality Act (popularly termed the McCarran-Walter, or simply the McCarran, Act), which became effective on December 24, 1952.[28] According to this act, only the applicant who fulfills the legal prerequisites and comes within the quota is entitled to admission. The quotas were computed by means of a complicated method, taking into account the respective numbers of immigrants prior to 1920. The Swiss quota, amounting to 1,698,[29] is relatively high and is actually filled by applicants meeting the legal requirements.[30]

In Switzerland, immigration is left to the discretion of the federal

---

[25] Burckhardt, *op. cit. supra* note 23, at §1864.

[26] 3 G. H. Hackworth, *Digest of International Law* (1942), 696.

[27] Act of May 26, 1924, 43 Stat. 153.

[28] "An Act to revise the laws relating to immigration, naturalization, and nationality; and for other purposes" of June 27, 1952, 66 Stat. 163, 8 U.S.C. §1101 (1952). See commentary by Besterman, 8 U.S.C.A. 1-91; E. Lowenstein, *The Alien and the Immigration Law* (1958); F. Auerbach, *The Immigration Laws of the United States* (1955); S. Kansas, *Immigration and Nationality Act* (1953; supp. 1955).

[29] Proclamation No. 2980 of July 2, 1952, 66 Stat. c36, 8 U.S.C.A. §1151, note.

[30] Swiss immigration amounted to 1627 in 1955 and to 1750 in 1956 (perhaps including some non-quota immigrants). *Statistical Abstract of the United States* (1957), 93.

and cantonal authorities.[31] Foreign labor is accepted to a considerable extent on a temporary basis because of Switzerland's industrial
needs, but perpetual immigrants are admitted only on a small scale.[32]

C. *Right to Work*[33]

In the United States, the right to work and to do business is safe-
guarded by the Federal Constitution, whose protection every lawful
immigrant enjoys fully. The Constitution as construed by the courts
forbids discrimination against aliens in employment and trade.[34] This
favorable approach does not extend to professions requiring a special
education (such as medicine, dentistry or law), which may — and in
fact usually are — reserved to American citizens by state law;[35] in
numerous cases it is sufficient that the petitioner has applied for citizenship.[36] Also, the state's power to keep aliens out of "public works"
has been upheld by the Supreme Court, even in the teeth of an Italian
treaty phrased more favorably to aliens than the Swiss treaty.[37] However, state laws denying aliens a chauffeur's[38] or barber's[39] license
have been held unconstitutional.

The restrictive power of a state is limited even within its "pro-

---

[31] F. Fleiner and Z. Giacometti, *Schweizerisches Bundesstaatsrecht* (1949),
ch. 3.

[32] According to *Statistisches Jahrbuch der Schweiz* (1956), 126, "first" per-
mission for limited sojourn was granted in 1956 to 269,357 seasonal (non-pro-
fessional) workers. The corresponding figures for 1946 and 1951 were 48,635 and
136,775 respectively. *Id.* at 127. These figures do not include tourists.

[33] A general comparative inquiry is offered by Lenhoff, "The Right to Work:
Here and Abroad", 46 Ill. L. Rev. 669 (1951).

[34] *Cf.* Note, "1947-48 Term of the Supreme Court: The Alien's Right to
Work", 49 Colum. L. Rev. 257 (1949).

[35] The legislation involved is subject to changes, hence earlier studies like
Brouse, "State Laws Barring Aliens from Professions and Occupations", 3 Immigration and Naturalization Service Monthly Rev. 281 (1948) can no longer
be relied upon. International Institute for the Unification of Private Law, *Com-
pilation of Laws on the Legal Status of Aliens. United States. Local Legislation*
(1953), 229-324, gives a good survey of the pertinent laws in the United Laws.
New York requires citizenship for attorneys, bank directors, embalmers, fish
and game guides, liquor dealers, maritime ship masters, pilots and engineers,
private detectives and race-track employees.

[36] In New York State, this rule applies to architects, billiard-room operators,
certified pubic accountants, certified shorthand reporters, dentists, pharmacists,
physicians including osteopaths and physiotherapists, real estate brokers and
salesmen, registered nurses, public-school teachers, professional engineers, land
surveyors and liquor dealers.

[37] Heim v. McCall, 239 U.S. 175 (1915).

[38] Magnani v. Harnett, 282 N.Y. 619, 25 N.E.2d 395 (1940), *cert. denied,*
310 U.S. 642 (1940).

[39] Templar v. Michigan State Board of Examiners, 131 Mich. 253, 90 N.W.
1058 (1902); State *ex rel.* Quisor v. Ellis, 184 P.2d 860 (Ore. 1947).

prietary" sphere, to which the privileges of foreigners do not usually extend, as the Treaty of 1850 recognizes in article I, paragraph 2. On the basis of its prerogative in the proprietary sphere, California excluded the Japanese by statute from fishing in her tidal waters; but this statute was declared unconstitutional by the Supreme Court in words which clearly expressed a liberal attitude not confined to the fishery question.[40]

A problem arose involving the restrictive power of municipalities when early in this century some American municipalities, New York among them, required alien itinerant salesmen (including the Swiss) to obtain a license which was not demanded of Americans.[41] That provision is no longer in force.

There is no counterpart to this constitutional approach in Swiss law. Immigration into Switzerland is ordinarily permitted only for one definite type of work, usually as the employee of a named employer. Such employees are needed mainly by Swiss firms having some connection with this country or using American techniques. Swiss interest plays a decisive role in granting the "visum," and this places the immigrant in a rather insecure position, though the text of the visum is couched in general terms.

The protection of political and religious refugees has long been granted by Switzerland, and has proved efficient and successful, especially with respect to the Huguenots in the sixteenth and seventeenth centuries.[42] Nevertheless, for reasons easy to understand, Switzerland lacks the tradition which is symbolically expressed in the inviting salute of the Statue of Liberty. The attitude of the Swiss authorities, for instance, was extremely reserved toward refugees from Hitler's persecution, who were not even permitted to earn money during their sojourn.[43]

A further instance of Swiss nationalism is afforded by the decree of the Swiss Federal Council of November 3, 1944 reserving the book-publishing business to Swiss citizens in order to protect it from excessive foreign influence (*Überfremdung*).[44] This motivation is difficult to reconcile, as far as Americans are concerned, with the spirit of the Treaty of 1850.

---

[40] Oyama v. California, 332 U.S. 633 (1948); Takahashi v. Fish & Game Commission, 334 U.S. 410 (1948).

[41] Burckhardt, *op. cit. supra* note 23, at §1863.

[42] See, *e.g.*, K. Mayer, *The Population of Switzerland* (1952), 220 ff.

[43] This serious occurrence led to a most careful and impressive report to the Federal Council (*Bundesrat*) by Prof. Dr. Karl Ludwig. See *Die Flüchtlingspolitik der Schweiz in den Jahren 1933 bis 1955* (Bundesrat Publication Zu 7347, 1957) for this report and the reply by Mr. E. von Steiger, a member of the Council. See especially pages 28-31, 52, 53, 54 and 60-72. See also Mayer, *op. cit. supra* note 42, at 240.

[44] AS 60, 715; BS 4, 256. See also SchwJbIntR 2, 205 (1945).

D. Naturalization and Dual Citizenship

The difference in approach is even more striking with respect to the acquisition of citizenship or naturalization. Under Swiss law, citizenship is granted by cooperation of the federal, cantonal and communal authorities.[45] The grant is discretionary, the canton playing the most important role.[46] Here, again, Swiss authorities are influenced by their strong feeling (more understandable in this case) against "Überfremdung."[47] The number of Swiss naturalizations is therefore small.[48] Still, there are some circumstances leading to the acquisition of Swiss citizenship without naturalization: (a) Legitimate children of a Swiss father and illegitimate children of a Swiss mother are Swiss citizens even if born abroad;[49] (b) A woman who marries a Swiss citizen acquires Swiss nationality.[50] Renunciation of Swiss citizenship is permitted only for dual citizens over twenty years of age, with the approval of the cantonal government.[51]

The American attitude is fundamentally different. Naturalization is granted in the United States by the courts, primarily the federal courts of first resort (district courts) on the basis of detailed statutory requirements set forth by the McCarran Act.[52] First of all, the immigrant must have resided in the United States for at least five years.[53] Among the other prerequisites are good moral character, knowledge of English, and lack of membership in Communist organizations. The Federal Government cooperates with the courts through its Immigration and Naturalization Service, which is subordinated to the Attorney General, but it has no discretion in naturalization matters, and state governments do not participate in the procedure. Swiss immigrants often avail themselves of the opportunity offered by this legisla-

---

[45] Fleiner and Giacometti, op. cit. supra note 31, ch. 3; Cohn, "The New Swiss Nationality Act", 2 Int'l & Comp. L. Q. 427 (1953).

[46] See the federal Law of September 29, 1952 on acquisition and loss of Swiss citizenship (Erwerb und Verlust des Schweizerbürgerrechts), AS 1952 (II), 1087, cited hereinafter as Law of 1952.

[47] Fleiner and Giacometti, op. cit. supra note 31, at 189.

[48] In 1956, 2,914 persons were naturalized under "easier" (erleichterte) conditions. Statistisches Jahrbuch der Schweiz (1956), 128.

[49] Law of 1952, art. 1.

[50] Constitution of 1874, art. 54(4).

[51] Law of 1952, art. 42. In 1956, 220 persons lost their citizenship in this manner. Statistisches Jahrbuch der Schweiz (1956), 133.

In addition, children born abroad of Swiss parents who were also born abroad lose their citizenship unless they declare their desire to retain it before reaching their twenty-second year. Law of 1952, art. 10.

[52] Supra note 28.

[53] A maximum of three years is required of an applicant who has married an American citizen and lived with him or her during this period. McCarran Act, §319(a), 8 U.S.C. §1430(a) (1952).

tion. Each person petitioning for naturalization must take an oath in open court to renounce and abjure all allegiance and fidelity to any foreign country of which he was a subject,[54] but this oath does not nullify Swiss citizenship under Swiss law. The Federal Council has power to cancel the Swiss citizenship of a person who, while possessing another citizenship, seriously injures the interest or the authority of Switzerland by his attitude,[55] but no instance is known where the oath referred to or any other aspect of American naturalization has caused such a cancellation.

In addition to naturalization, the old common law rule of *jus soli* renders children born in the United States citizens despite the Swiss nationality of their parents.[56]

In some respects, American naturalization is less stable than the Swiss: a naturalized person loses his citizenship by residing three years in the country of his birth or five years in any any other country.[57] This limitation, introduced in 1940,[58] is of special significance to Swiss citizens because of their homeward trend.

Nevertheless, dual American-Swiss citizenship is a frequent phenomenon in the United States.[59] Within the field of public international law, the resulting problems are reduced by a Swiss practice under which a Swiss citizen naturalized by and living in another country is not entitled to the rights and protection granted to Swiss citizens.[60] In the field of private international law, dual citizenship does not create many difficulties because the pertinent rules, American as well as Swiss, place the emphasis on domicile rather than nationality. Where citizenship is in point, the "dualist" will be con-

---

[54] *Id.* §337(a)(2), 8 U.S.C. §1448(a)(2) (1952). This requirement was introduced by the Act of March 2, 1929, §338(c), 45 Stat. 1512.

[55] Law of 1952, art. 48.

[56] McCarran Act, §301(a)(1), 8 U.S.C. §1401(a)(1) (1952).

[57] *Id.* §352, 8 U.S.C. §1484 (1952).

[58] Nationality Act of October 14, 1940, §338(c), 54 Stat. 1137.

[59] According to H. R. Christ in *Die Schweiz. Ein Nationales Jahrbuch* (1956), 35, there are in the United States a large number of American-Swiss dual citizens not registered with the Swiss consulates, estimated at 121,650 for the year 1954, whereas only about 12,000 were registered in that same year. On military grounds, Swiss law requires registration with the consulates of Swiss men from 20 to 60 years of age.

[60] Art. 6 of the Federal Law of June 25, 1903 on acquisition and renunciation of Swiss citizenship (*Erwerbung des Schweizerbürgerrechts und den Verzicht auf dasselbe*), AS 19, 690; BS 1, 101, a rule still followed although it was omitted and thus abrogated by the Law of 1952.

sidered by American courts as an American[61] and by Swiss courts as a Swiss.[62]

Nevertheless, serious questions may arise in the military field as the result of dual citizenship.[63] Swiss law restricts military service to Swiss citizens; hence, on this point, there is no problem for American citizens living in Switzerland. And there is little probability of their becoming Swiss citizens. However, in the United States, military service (between the ages of 18 and 35) has never been confined to citizens. Under article II of the Treaty of 1850, "citizens of one of the two countries, residing or established in the other, shall be free from personal military service." But what of the individual possessing dual citizenship? To meet this situation, a new treaty was concluded on American initiative in 1937.[64] It provided that a person possessing both American citizenship and Swiss nationality by birth and having his habitual residence in the State of his birth should not be "held liable" by the other State for military service. However, should the person stay in the other State for more than two years, this would create a presumption that the prior habitual residence had been abandoned. This means, practically, that the Swiss authorities would be entitled to demand military service of a dual American-Swiss citizen who had returned to Switzerland, but under the McCarran Act such service would cause loss of American citizenship.[65]

Military service has created difficulties in other respects. Gradually, and especially under the pressure of two World Wars, this country has developed a doctrine according to which naturalization will be denied to immigrants who have applied for relief from service in the armed forces. Jurisdiction of our federal courts extends also to this situation. In two cases, Swiss immigrants were granted naturalization

---

[61] Cf. Blair Holdings Corp. v. Rubinstein, 133 F. Supp. 496 (S.D.N.Y. 1955).

[62] See the Feldis case, infra note 94, at 316, and, regarding French-Swiss dual citizenship, Dobler v. Dobler, BGE 81(II) 495 (1955). A general discussion is offered by R. Feer, Die mehrfache Staatsangehörigkeit natürlicher Personen (thesis Zürich 1955). On dual citizenship in connection with art. VI of the Treaty of 1850, see infra page 28, and in connection with taxation, see arts. VI, VII and XI of the income tax convention, infra pages 68-70.

[63] R. Probst, Zwischenstaatliche Abgrenzung der Wehrpflicht (Abhandlungen zum Schweizerischen Recht, 313 N.F., 87 (1955); id., "International Demarcation of Compulsory Military Service", 45 Georgetown L. J. 60 (1956).

[64] 53 Stat. 1791; TS 943; 193 LNTS 181; AS 54, 854; BS 11, 588. Cases illustrating the difficulties leading to this treaty are found in 2 L. von Salis, Schweizerisches Bundesrecht (1903), 486.

[65] Sec. 349(a)(3), 8 U.S.C. §1481(a)(3) (1952).

by the courts after it had been denied by the government.[66] The immigrant plaintiffs had applied for and received relief from military service during World War II. The courts pointed out that they had acted in good faith, in the belief that their applications would not deprive them of their right to become American citizens — a belief induced by favorable statements of the Swiss Embassy (incidentally, an unusual diplomatic act). But the situation has changed. The McCarran Act specifically denies naturalization to those who have applied for relief from military service.[67] This legislative refusal of naturalization is not in conflict with the Treaty of 1850, which does not guarantee the right to become a citizen.[68] The lawful Swiss immigrant, although relieved from military duty and deprived of naturalization, still remains entitled to permanent residence in this country and — apart from the state restrictions mentioned above[69] — can freely choose his occupation as no American could do in Switzerland. Moreover, his wife would not be excluded from citizenship, and his children would be American citizens if born in this country.[70]

Unfortunately, however, there remains another serious difficulty. A Swiss citizen who had immigrated to the United States in 1954 requested and was granted relief from American military service the same year. Later he made a temporary trip to Switzerland, and it was decided that he had lost thereby his right to remain in the United States and that, having returned, he was to be deported.[71] This decision, it is believed, runs counter to the meaning of the Treaty of 1850 (which was not mentioned in the case), under which citizens

---

[66] Moser v. United States, 341 U.S. 41 (1951); Petition of Berini, 112 F. Supp. 837 (E.D.N.Y. 1953). See also Lehmann v. Acheson, 206 F. 2d 592 (3d Cir. 1953), where expatriation of a dual citizen born in this country was rejected though he had lived with his mother in Switzerland since the age of three and had served in the Swiss army before returning to the United States. Compare the Reitmann case, *infra* note 71. The cases are discussed by Domke in SJZ: 49, 324 (1953); 50, 288 (1954); 51, 328 (1955); 53, 234 (1957).

[67] McCarran Act, §315, 8 U.S.C. §1426 (1952). *Cf.* Petition of Mauderli, 122 F. Supp. 241 (N.D. Fla. 1954); In re Fleischmann's Petition, 141 F. Supp. 292 (S.D.N.Y. 1956) ("duress" no excuse); Petition of Oster, 287 P.2d 859 (Cal. App. 1955).

[68] As emphasized in the Oster case.

[69] *Supra* page 14.

[70] *Supra* page 17.

[71] Schenkel v. Landon, 133 F. Supp. 305 (D. Mass. 1955). (The plaintiff had based his claim on the assertion that his relief from military service was invalid, a weak argument outside the scope of our inquiry.) The savings clause of §405(a) of the McCarren Act, 8 U.S.C. §1101, note (1952), maintaining the validity of certain earlier acts, has been held not to prevent retroactive application of §315. Barber v. Rietmann [sic], 248 F.2d 118 (9th Cir. 1957), *reversing* Application of Reitmann, 148 F. Supp. 556 (N.D. Cal. 1956). The treaty was not mentioned in either case.

of one country shall be free from personal military service in the other (article II, paragraph 1). The denial of any temporary trip abroad would constitute a serious penalty for obtaining this dispensation, and would infringe on the liberty of the Swiss immigrant to "come, go [and] sojourn temporarily" (article I, paragraph 1, second sentence). Observance of treaty provisions is expressly required by the McCarran Act itself.[72]

E. *Power to Acquire and Dispose of Property*

Article V, paragraph 1 of the Treaty of 1850 authorizes citizens of either country to dispose of and to inherit personal property. The disposition may be carried out "by sale, testament, donation, or in any other manner." By the same provision, national treatment is guaranteed with respect to inheritance taxes and other transfer charges. Leaving aside inheritance taxes, which were specifically regulated by the Treaty of 1951,[73] the rules listed above have little importance, since they only follow what is today the law and usage for matters of personal property in all countries of Western civilization.

The situation is entirely different as regards real property, however, at least in the United States. There, real property has always been subject to state law, and most states have followed the English tradition which, since the time of feudalism, has severely restricted the power of aliens to own land. This attitude was one of the main obstacles to the Treaty of 1850, and the negotiating governments finally had to make concessions on this score. Article V, paragraph 2 declares the general rules of paragraph 1 applicable to real estate only in those American states or Swiss cantons "in which foreigners shall be entitled to hold or inherit real estate." In Switzerland all cantons belong to this group, but where an American state takes a different view of the matter, article V, paragraph 3 of the treaty provides that a Swiss heir or other Swiss successor shall be permitted to sell the real property within the term accorded by the law of that state. In the latter case, he is at liberty to withdraw and export the proceeds of the sale without being subjected to charges which the state authorities would not impose upon "an inhabitant." These provisions were liberally construed in 1879 by the Supreme Court of the United States

---

[72] Sec. 357, 8 U.S.C. §1489 (1952). The same problem may arise with respect to the discretion of the Attorney General in permitting re-entry. §223(b), 8 U.S.C. §1203(b) (1952).

The question here discussed may affect the rights of an American citizen residing in Switzerland, who may be denied a visa for a temporary trip to another country in retaliation for the United States' position as expressed in the Schenkel case.

[73] *Infra* page 45.

in the important case of *Hauenstein v. Lynham*.[74] A Swiss citizen had died intestate in 1861 or 1862 leaving valuable real estate in Virginia, the state of his last domicile. Since Virginia at the time did not permit aliens to inherit real property, and since there were no American heirs, the Virginia escheator sold the property. A suit brought much later by the Swiss heirs against the escheator for the proceeds of the sale was dismissed by the Virginia courts on the ground that Virginia law did not provide for such a claim.[75] The Supreme Court reversed. It construed article V of the Treaty of 1850 as granting the successors of the deceased Swiss citizen an absolute right to sell the real property, any state law to the contrary notwithstanding. Moreover, since Virginia had not "accorded" a "term" for the sale of the property, the Supreme Court held that no time limit could apply in such a case. The escheator was directed to pay the proceeds to the Swiss heirs, and was permitted to keep only his usual fees for the sale.

Two years earlier, treaty protection had also been granted by the Supreme Court of the District of Columbia (a court of first resort) to a Swiss testamentary successor to real property left in the District by an American (formerly Swiss) decedent.[76] However, in 1909, by a decision of an Indiana appellate court, Swiss heirs lost real property because they had not transferred it within five years to an American citizen, as required at the time by Indiana law.[77] There is also a report according to which a California estate was lost because the Swiss heir had been absent from California for five years following the acquisition of the estate, without filing a claim thereto as required by California law.[78]

But today these cases have little significance. State laws have changed widely during this century in favor of aliens and therefore of non-naturalized Swiss citizens, whether living within or without

---

[74] 100 U.S. 483 (1879). The Supreme Court declared a treaty to be the "supreme law of the land" and hence superior to state law; it also stated its preference for the "liberal" rather than the restrictive interpretation of a treaty.

In an earlier case involving the Treaty of 1850, the Court did not reach consideration of the merits, holding merely that ratification of the treaty did not have a retroactive effect where it operated on individual rather than governmental rights. Haver v. Yaker, 9 Wall. 32 (1869).

[75] Hauenstein v. Lynham, 69 Va. 62 (1877).

[76] Jost v. Jost, 12 D.C. 487 (1882).

[77] Lehman v. State, 45 Ind. App. 330, 88 N.E. 365 (1909). The expropriation was carried out ten years after the death of the decedent; the successors kept what they had earned from the land during that period.

[78] Burckhardt, *op. cit. supra* note 23, at §1860, where the Lehman case is also discussed.

the United States.[79] For instance, New York[80] and California[81] have abolished the incapacities of aliens regarding real property, while in Pennsylvania the restriction only applies to land exceeding 5,000 acres or yielding a net annual income of $20,000.[82]

Further questions may arise with respect to acquisition and disposal of property[83] under international sales contracts. A decision of the commercial court of Zürich dated June 16, 1950 involved the sale of goods by a Swiss firm to an American company which requested damages for quality flaws.[84] Although the correspondence between the parties had been carried out in English and the price was to be paid in dollars, Swiss law was held controlling because the underlying facts were connected mainly with Switzerland.[85] Other American-Swiss cases in this sphere (or generally in the contracts field[86]) are not known.[87]

---

[79] A careful synthesis and analysis of these laws is presented in 1 R. B. Powell, *The Law of Real Property* (1949; cum. supp. 1956), §§101-109.

[80] N. Y. Real Property Law, §§10, 11 and 15.

[81] The California Alien Land Law restricting acquisition of land by aliens was finally repealed in 1957 following various legislative measures short of repeal. Cal. Stat. 1957, CXXXVII.

[82] Purdon's Pa. Stat. Ann., tit. 68, §§28, 32, 51 and 53-60.

[83] Transfer of chattels is governed by the law of the country where the transfer takes place, a rule applicable especially to negotiable instruments or other commercial papers tainted by forgery but transferred to a bona fide recipient. *Cf.* United States v. Arnhold & S. Bleichroeder, Inc., 96 F. Supp. 240 (S.D.N.Y. 1951) (transfer of postal money orders); see also Eisler v. Soskin, 272 App. Div. 894, 71 N.Y.S.2d 682 (1st Dep't 1947), *aff'd*, 297 N.Y. 841, 78 N.E.2d 862 (1948) (transfer of money to gratuitous bailee). Swiss law takes the same view; see, *e.g.*, 2 A. F. Schnitzer, *Handbuch des Internationalen Privatrechts* (4th ed. 1958), 565.

[84] BlZR 1950 No. 199.

[85] In this respect, the court followed the approach of this writer in *Deutsches Internationales Privatrecht* (1932), 22 *ff.* It referred also to the widespread knowledge of foreign languages by Swiss merchants and their willingness to correspond in English.

[86] A general discussion of conflict rules regarding contracts cannot be offered within the framework of the present study, but it may be mentioned that rules useful to the practitioner can hardly be derived from the present status of American and Swiss cases. Express contractual agreements on the applicability of Swiss law or of the law of the pertinent American state would have a good chance of judicial approval. This writer has presented his views in the work cited *supra* note 84, at §34 *ff.*, as well as in his *Principles of Private International Law* (1943; German ed., *Grundzüge des Internationalen Privatrechts*, 1952), §16 *ff.*

[87] Conflicts problems on a Swiss sale of goods to a New York firm also appear in Productos A. G. v. Ruckstuhl, BGE 81 (II) 175 (1955), but the decision was not based upon them. In Fickel v. Codman, BGE 20, 648 (1894), a married woman domiciled in Pennsylvania had purchased carpets in Zürich, but disclaimed liability because under Pennsylvania law she was incapable of contracting. This defense was held material. However, since 1907, Swiss law on capacity is controlling in such a case. NAG art. 7b (*infra* page 79). On the American side, incapacity of married women has been almost completely abolished. See, *e.g.*, G. L. Clark, *Domestic Relations* (1954), 75.

Finally, a minor point in American-Swiss contracts was dealt with by the 1924 Brussels Convention for the Unification of Certain Rules Relating to (Ocean) Bills of Lading, which has been adhered to by both countries.[88] The right of sea carriers to restrict their obligations toward the holders of bills of lading was limited thereby.

F. *Inheritance*

Article V of the Treaty of 1850 is concerned with the protection of acquired property; but how such property is to be acquired depends primarily on the applicable legal system. In this respect, choice of law is of the greatest importance as regards inheritance, both intestate and testamentary. Contrary to the common law approach which favors liberty of testation, the testator under a civil law system has no power to dispose of his property by will without regard for his wife and next of kin, who are granted an indefeasible inheritance right (*légitime* or *Pflichtteil*) amounting to a sizable fraction (up to three-quarters) of the estate.[89] Under Swiss law the *légitime* is substantial and extends even to brothers and sisters.[90]

The question of how to determine the applicable law is dealt with in article VI of the treaty. It reads as follows:

> Any controversy that may arise among the claimants to the same succession, as to whom the property shall belong, shall be decided according to the laws and by the judges of the country in which the property is situated.

Taken literally, this provision would imply that whenever the property is dispersed over several countries each piece — however small the pieces and however numerous — will be subject to the law of the country where it is located. Obviously this cannot be the real meaning. At the time when the treaty was concluded, there existed in Europe as well as in this country a familiar theory which considered *movables* legally situated at their owner's domicile (*mobilia personam sequuntur*). Application of this theory leads to a reasonable interpretation of article VI: the movables left by the decedent are governed

---

[88] 51 Stat. 233; TS 931; 120 LNTS 155; AS 1954, 758; BS 7, 543, 565. On the American side, it was substantially incorporated into the Bills of Lading (Pomerene) Act of August 29, 1916, 39 Stat. 538, as amended March 4, 1927, 44 Stat. 1540, 49 U.S.C. §§81-124 (1952); *cf.* S. Dor, *Bills of Lading Clauses and the Brussels International Convention [Hague Rules]* (1956); A. W. Knauth, *The American Law of Ocean Bills of Lading* (4th ed. 1953), 46. It may be mentioned that there are also some Swiss seafaring companies; *cf. Statistisches Jahrbuch der Schweiz* (1956), 267.

[89] Illegitimate children are legal successors of their fathers neither under American nor under Swiss law. *Cf.* Estate of Rougeron, N.Y.L.J. Mar. 11, 1957, p. 8, col. 7 (Surr. Ct.)

[90] The *légitime* is regulated to a large extent by cantonal law up to the present day. ZGB art. 472.

by the law and jurisdiction of the place where he had his last domicile; real property remains under the law and jurisdiction of the *rei sitae.* This is in accordance with the common law tradition as well as with the fundamental distinction between personal and real property made in article V. True, the Federal Council tried to have the treaty establish the law of the last domicile as the basis of the entire succession, including real property, and to add some other conflicts provisions, *e.g.,* on the law governing the form of wills.[91] But the Council did not succeed. In a message to the Swiss Federal Assembly on December 3, 1850,[92] shortly after the treaty was signed, the Council asserted that both parties were "very certain that article VI would be interpreted as placing the entire estate, both movables and immovables, under control of the law of the last domicile." Yet there is no corresponding American statement; and this fact would be sufficient to deprive the assertion of any binding effect in the interpretation of the treaty. Moreover, the assertion refers to a version of article VI which was later changed.[93]

As a result, American real property left by a Swiss citizen is subject to American law and jurisdiction, and Swiss real property left by an American citizen is subject to Swiss law and jurisdiction; personal property is subject to the law and jurisdiction of the last domicile. The leading decision was rendered by the Swiss Federal Tribunal

---

[91] Regarding the form of wills, which apparently is not affected by the treaty, the state rules on probate of wills give the basic answer to the conflicts problems involved. Within the state concerned, a foreigner may execute a will in the form provided by the state law, but in New York a testament will be probated if it is executed in accordance with the law either of the place where executed or of the testator's last domicile, provided the will is in writing and subscribed by the testator (Decedent Estate Law §23). California recognizes, for personal property only, foreign testaments meeting, with respect to their form, the requirements of the law of the testator's last domicile (West's Ann. Cal. Codes, vol. 52, §26) and Pennsylvania grants probate to a will "proved in a foreign country, according to the laws thereof" (Purdon's Pa. Stat. Ann., tit. 20, §1882). See, generally, Yiannopoulos, "Wills of Movables in American International Conflicts Law: A Critique of the Domiciliary 'Rule'", 46 Calif. L. Rev. 185 (1958). Regarding American real property, under a common law tradition, observance of the law of the situs is required for the form of testaments not only in California but in many other states. Swiss private international law in this matter is federal and relatively simple; see NAG art. 24 (*infra* page 80) which, according to art. 32, applies "by analogy" to foreigners, "home canton" thereby obviously being replaced by "home state".

[92] 5 Miller, *op. cit. supra* note 1, at 865-875.

[93] The Message states that in art. VI of the treaty, signed on November 25, 1850, the words "(whether personal or real)" had been added to the term "property". Nevertheless, the words in parentheses were struck out by the United States Senate on March 7, 1851, and this version, together with other changes, was accepted by Switzerland in 1855. See 5 Miller, *op. cit. supra* note 1, at 878.

on May 5, 1898 in the *Feldis* case.[94] A Swiss citizen domiciled in Switzerland had left personal as well as real property in Switzerland and in New York. On the basis of article VI, the Tribunal assumed jurisdiction over the movables as well as over the Swiss (but not the American) real property. As emphasized by the Tribunal, two of its previous judgments had taken the same view — namely, *In re Wohlwend* of November 24, 1883[95] and *In re Michael* of December 13, 1894.[96] The *Wohlwend* case, which quotes extensively from the 1850 Message of the Federal Council, was merely concerned with movables left by a Swiss citizen in the United States where he had his last domicile; hence, the Tribunal disclaimed its own jurisdiction. Exactly the same view was taken in 1885 by the Appellate and Cassation Court of Bern regarding movables and immovables left both in the United States and Switzerland by a Swiss citizen domiciled in Switzerland;[97] Bern jurisdiction was denied only concerning the American real property. And in 1940 the Appellate Court of Ticino[98] claimed jurisdiction over inheritance of Ticino real property left by an American domiciled in California. The decision was based on article VI of the treaty as well as on NAG article 28.[99]

All Swiss writers agree with this judicial interpretation of article VI.[100]

This simple and fair solution of the problem has recently been complicated by the decision of a New York surrogate, *In re Schneider's Estate*.[101] An American citizen of Swiss descent, whose last domicile was New York, left real property in Switzerland. The surrogate applied New York law on a "renvoi" theory to that property—or rather, to the proceeds of its sale which had been remitted to New York. The decedent's widow and next of kin were thereby deprived of the *légitime* granted them by Swiss law. The court's reasoning ran as follows: Swiss law subjects succession to the whole estate, personal or real, to the law of the last domicile, hence in this case to New York law, with the result that if the real estate is situated in Switzerland, New York law applies on the basis of renvoi; if it is situated

---

[94] In Sachen Gemeinde Feldis und Konsorten, BGE 24(I) 312 (1898). The Feldis holding on movables was approved in Nussle v. Ros, *infra* note 117.

[95] In Sachen Wohlwend, BGE 9, 507 (1883).

[96] Not published.

[97] 2 F. Meili, *Das internationale Civil- und Handelsrecht* (1902), 206.

[98] *In re* Lanella, Rep. 73, 461 (1940).

[99] *Infra* page 80.

[100] M. Guldener, *Das Internationale und Interkantonale Civilprozessrecht der Schweiz* (1952), 122, n. 2; H. Lewald, "'Renvoi Revisited' in Fragen des Verfahrens- und Kollisionsrechtes", *Festschrift für Hans Fritzsche* (1952), 165; P. Anliker, *Die Erbrechtlichen Verhältnisse der Ausländer in der Schweiz* (1933), 115.

[101] 96 N.Y.S.2d 652 (1950).

in New York, New York law applies as the *lex rei sitae*, in accordance with the American conflicts doctrine.

The renvoi doctrine cannot, however, be employed contrary to the conflicts norm supplied by a treaty. Under article VI, the succession to real property is to be governed by the "laws" of the country where the real property is situated, and this obviously means internal laws. Furthermore, the court misinterpreted the Swiss decisions, which actually hold the law of the last domicile applicable under article VI *only in the case of personal property.*[102]

The opinion is perplexing in another respect as well. The surrogate discusses for more than four pages the general theories on the law of the situs and on renvoi, which was not referred to by the parties. He then adds that his "attention has been first called to the Swiss-American Treaty of 1850," to which, as well as to the *Wohlwend* and *Feldis* cases, a shorter discussion is granted. An explanation of this strange reasoning is provided by several references to "Renvoi Revisited," an article which had been published by Dean Griswold of the Harvard Law School (incidentally, with no consideration of the Swiss or any similar problem).[103] As a result of this over-theoretical approach, the opinion has aroused worldwide attention such as has rarely been paid to a conflicts decision, especially one rendered by a court of first resort. [104] The criticism raised soon after publication of the case caused the Swiss party to apply for reargument in the surrogate's court. The court, however, insisted upon its prior ruling, pointing out that in the *Feldis* case the Swiss Tribunal had not claimed jurisdiction over New York real property. But the court did not mention the fact that the Tribunal had assumed jurisdiction over the *Swiss* real

---

[102] The surrogate also cites the following remark made by this writer about the Wohlwend case in "American-Swiss Private International Law", 47 Colum. L. Rev. 186, 196 (1947): "Relying on the Message of 1850, the Tribunal did not distinguish between movables and immovables". But this writer had added that the Bern Court in 1885, and later the Federal Tribunal in the Feldis case, took a different view. This the surrogate did not mention.

[103] 51 Harv. L. Rev. 1165 (1938).

[104] In addition to the first edition of this study, at 21 *ff.*, striking criticism has been presented by Lewald, a leading Swiss writer in this field, *supra* note 100, at 173 *ff.;* and on the common law side, by Falconbridge in an extensive analysis of renvoi in *Essays on the Conflict of Laws* (2d ed. 1954), 236 *ff.;* by Zweigert in Zeitschrift für ausländisches und internationales Privatrecht 16, 620 (1951) [with German translation of the opinion]; by Wengler in Neue Juristische Wochenschrift 4, 300 (1951) and by others; see 50 Colum. L. Rev. 862 (1950) and 64 Harv. L. Rev. 166 (1950). Ehrenzweig, "Interstate and International Conflicts Law: A Pleas for Segregation", 41 Minn. L. Rev. 717, 728, n. 59 (1957) calls it "the widely criticized case".

Reports which do not take a critical point of view are found in 26 N.Y.U.L. Rev. 201 (1951); 3 Int'l L. Q. 268 (1951) (assenting); 77 Journal du Droit International 976 (1950) [with French and German translations of the opinion]; and 3 Revue Hellénique de Droit International 310 (1950).

Rabel, in a brief reference, expressed doubt. 4 Int'l L. Q. 406 (1951).

property, which was the decisive point. There is hardly any danger that such elimination of Swiss law will be followed by other courts.[105]

The application of article VI has, of course, some effects on Swiss internal law, as for instance, in the computation of a Swiss *légitime*. The value of American realty must be excluded if the decedent, whether American or Swiss, had his last domicile in Switzerland.

Far more significant are the repercussions of article VI on the Swiss conflict rules, especially on those laid down in the NAG. Article 28 of this statute provides that, in the absence of a treaty, the real property of Swiss citizens domiciled abroad, whether or not they are subject to foreign law, is governed by the law and jurisdiction of their cantonal home (*Heimat-Kanton*) rather than that of the canton where the immovable is located. However, the ZGB of 1907 (third part) has on the whole replaced cantonal law with respect to inheritance, although cantonal law is still of primary importance with respect to jurisdiction and procedure. More important, under NAG article 22(2), Swiss citizens may by testament[106] subject the inheritance of their future estate to the law of their canton. This rule is by "analogy". (*"entsprechend"*) applicable to foreigners domiciled in Switzerland (article 32), a matter of special importance to Americans who have taken or intend to take their domicile in Switzerland. By the "analogous" application of article 22(2), they may escape the stringent Swiss statutory provisions on the *légitime* and may preserve their American liberty of testation. However, a question arises whether under article VI of the Treaty of 1850 they can enjoy this liberty only in regard to American real estate, while their other property would remain subject to the law of their Swiss domicile. This was the view taken in 1911, in response to a query of the American Embassy, by the Swiss Federal Council, under the reservation that the ultimate decision would rest with the courts.[107] I doubt that the courts will follow the Council.[108] Application of the Swiss law of inheritance under the treaty includes, it is believed, the Swiss provisions permitting a foreign testator voluntarily to adopt his own national law. Otherwise American citi-

---

[105] Like the unfortunate Tallmadge case, 109 Misc. 696, 181 N.Y. Supp. 336 (Surr. Ct. 1919), the Schneider case illustrates the overemphasis on theoretical concepts often found in the literature of private international law; compare this writer, *op. cit. supra* note 89, at 102.

[106] Or by an "inheritance contract" (*Erbvertrag*).

[107] Statement of November 22, 1911, in Burckhardt, *op. cit. supra* note 23, at §1610.

[108] The Council probably relied on the not very definite opinion of Meili, *op. cit. supra* note 97, at 207, followed without further inquiry by Petitpierre, "Le Droit applicable à la succession des étrangers domiciliés en Suisse", *Recueil de Travaux offert par la Faculté de droit de l'Université de Neuchâtel à la Société Suisse des juristes* (1929), 239.

zens would be discriminated against as compared with other non-Swiss citizens residing in Switzerland, and such discrimination would run counter to the spirit of the treaty.

Hence, an American domiciled in Switzerland may by will adopt the law of that state which is the equivalent of a *Heimat-Kanton*. Now American state laws lack a concept equivalent to that of Swiss cantonal citizenship, but the "analogous" application of the Swiss statute would lead to the law of the American state where the testator had his or her last residence, "residence" being the closest relationship to a state, sometimes called "citizenship" in state statutes.[109] However, American courts confronted with such an American will might be influenced by their inclination to give effect, by interpretation or construction, to the intention of the testator.[110] The laws of the state of the testator's birth may sometimes appear to be the most adequate.

Under New York law,[111] a testator not domiciled in New York may direct by his will that his testamentary dispositions be construed and regulated by New York law, but this rule is incompatible with article VI of the treaty if the testator was domiciled in Switzerland. In such a case liberty to choose the law governing the will can be derived if at all only from Swiss law.[112]

This approach must be taken, it is believed, even in the case of the decedent's dual citizenship, because article VI is based on the law of the decedent's last domicile. Only if that law should refer to nationality in one or another point would the "dualist" be considered by the court to this extent as a citizen of the country where the court is located.[113] Still, the question is of little practical significance.

Quite frequently the treaty has been overlooked by American courts. Thus, in a case decided by a New York surrogate,[114] the testator, domiciled in Switzerland, executed in New York in 1934 a will subjecting his New York property to New York law; after his death

---

[109] See, *e.g.*, 7 *Words and Phrases* (1952), 255. In fact, the Fourteenth Amendment to the United States Constitution refers to American citizens as "citizens * * * of the State wherein they reside". A similar approach has been taken by Swiss courts, *infra* note 218.

[110] E. E. Cheatham, H. F. Goodrich, E. N. Griswold and W. L. M. Reese, *Cases and Materials on Conflict of Laws* (4th ed. 1957), 713. This trend appears even in the judicial interpretation of testamentary grants. See *In re* Mansbendel's Estate, *infra* note 203.

[111] Decedent Estate Law §47. This provision is applicable regardless of an opposite conflict norm of the law of the domicile. Matter of Cook, 204 Misc. 704, 123 N.Y.S. 2d 568 (Surr. Ct. 1953), *aff'd*, 283 App. Div. 1047, 131 N.Y.S. 2d 882 (1st Dep't 1954).

[112] *Supra* page 24.

[113] As indicated in the Feldis case, *supra* note 94.

[114] Matter of Hug, 201 Misc. 709, 107 N.Y.S. 2d 664 (Surr. Ct. 1949).

the surrogate placed that property under a New York administrator who disposed of it. Apparently the testator was a Swiss citizen. To what extent the will was valid in that case would depend on whether and how far it infringed on claims of *légitimes* according to Swiss law applicable under the treaty; but neither the treaty nor Swiss law was considered by the court. In another case,[115] the surrogate, confronted with the intestate inheritance from a Swiss citizen domiciled in Switzerland, held Swiss law applicable. The opinion cites several provisions of the Swiss Civil Code, one of which (article 733) refers to immovables—the realty involved in the case obviously being Swiss. But under the treaty how could the court assume jurisdiction in such a situation? The short record does not give an explanation. Again, there is no reference to the treaty. Swiss law was also held by the surrogate to govern a nuncupative will executed in German by an American citizen domiciled in Geneva.[116] This ruling is in accord with both common law and the treaty which, however, is not mentioned in the record.[117]

Of course, the treaty does not apply to estates of persons domiciled in the United States or Switzerland who are citizens of neither country. A relevant American case[118] is concerned with the estate of the celebrated Austrian 'cellist, Feuermann, who in 1938 executed his will in Zürich, then his domicile. He later shifted his domicile to New York, where he died in 1942. The will directed that his widow should be placed in the most advantageous position possible under Swiss law or, in case they were no longer domiciled in Switzerland, in the most advantageous position to be found "under the law then applicable to us." The surrogate pointed out that New York law was therefore controlling; and the whole estate ($33,000 from the sale of Feuermann's Stradivarius 'cello) was assigned to the widow. Under Swiss law, the child born after Feuermann's death would have been the main beneficiary, regardless of the testator's will. The decision which, of course, has nothing to do with renvoi, is convincing.

Another New York case deals with a will executed in New York by a German who died later in Switzerland where he had his last resi-

---

[115] Matter of Lullin, N.Y.L.J., Jan. 31, 1956, p. 11, col. 4 (Surr. Ct.).

[116] Matter of Batsholts, 188 Misc. 867, 66 N.Y.S. 2d 358 (Surr. Ct. 1946), *aff'd*, 67 N.Y.S. 2d 687 (App. Div., 1st Dep't, 1947). Other cases ignoring the treaty are referred to *infra* page 32.

[117] Delivery of movables inherited according to the law applicable under the treaty, and generally rights based on "possession", will be enforced in a different way — that is, by the court and under the law of the place where the movables are situated, Nussle v. Ros, BGE 43(I) 77 (1917).

[118] *In re* Feuermann's Will, 47 N.Y.S. 2d 738 (Surr. Ct. 1944).

dence.[119] Under article 24 of the Decedent Estate Law of the State of New York, the construction of a will is not affected by a change in the testator's residence made after the execution of the will; hence the will was properly interpreted according to New York law.[120] Finally, we might mention a Pennsylvania case concerned with the will of a wealthy American citizen domiciled in Switzerland.[121] In his will, executed in Switzerland with the help of a Swiss attorney, he directed that his widow should receive the *légitime* "as provided by the law of my country" (meaning Pennsylvania, the law of which allows the widow to take her intestate portion contrary to the husband's will). He left personal and real property in Pennsylvania. With a strong minority dissent, the suit was dismissed on the grounds that the widow was mentally ill and that her guardian had no power to claim the *légitime* for her. Had the widow been of Swiss nationality, the Treaty of 1850 would have been applicable and the Pennsylvania court would have lacked jurisdiction except as regarded the real estate. But the very elaborate opinion mentioned neither the nationality of the widow nor the treaty.

On the Swiss side, a surprising view, in cases where the treaty is not involved, has been taken with respect to Swiss real property. Under the general rule of NAG article 22, inheritance is subject to the law of the decedent's last domicile. But under article 28 of the same statute, Swiss real estate remains under Swiss law unless a treaty provides to the contrary. What, then, in this situation, is the result of the "analogous" application of the statute to foreigners domiciled in Switzerland, as required by NAG article 32? The Superior Court of Zürich considered inheritance of Swiss real property in the case of a Polish decedent as being controlled by Polish law.[122] A similar approach was taken in 1939 by the Swiss Real Property Registration Office (*Grundbuchamt*) regarding Swiss realty left by a Russian last domiciled in New York. New York law was held applicable to the succession.[123] This seems to be an exaggerated expansion of the domi-

---

[119] *In re* Fingerhut's Estate, 85 N.Y.S. 2d 716 (Surr. Ct. 1948). The German nationality is merely presumed above. The estate had been seized by the Alien Property Custodian. A different enemy nationality — Austrian, for instance — would not have changed the outcome.

[120] The New York will of a Belgian who had died in Switzerland was considered in Estate of De Bitche, 207 Misc. 237, 136 N.Y.S. 2d 566 (Surr. Ct. 1954). The validity of a transfer of his New York bank account was questioned, the letter written by him in Switzerland having been received by the New York bank after his death. New York law was applied with no reference to Swiss law.

[121] Harris Estate, 351 Pa. 368, 41 A. 2d 715 (1945).

[122] Superior Court of Zürich, June 6, 1935, BIZR 1935 No. 124.

[123] Statement of July 7, 1939, Verwaltungsentscheide der Bundesbehörden 13, 49, n. 32, cited by Lewald, *op. cit. supra* note 100, at n. 27.

cile doctrine; moreover, a renvoi from American to Swiss law would have been appropriate under that doctrine.

Regarding the administration of estates, American and Swiss law reflect a fundamental difference between common and civil law. Under Swiss law the whole of a decedent's estate, including the right to possession, passes by a kind of legal fiction to the heirs at the moment of the decedent's death.[124] There is no administration of estates except in a few extraordinary situations, particularly where an heir is permanently absent from the jurisdiction without having named an authorized attorney, but this administration is lawful only insofar as it is necessary in the heir's interest. Creditors are taken care of by a different institution, the "official liquidation" of the estate, a proceeding conducted by a liquidator appointed and supervised by the cantonal authority.[125] Again, it is only under narrowly defined prerequisites that a creditor can obtain the official liquidation, namely (1) that there is good reason for apprehending that payment will not be made otherwise; (2) that despite the creditor's demand, the heir or administrator neither discharges the debt nor gives security for it; (3) that no more than three months have elapsed since the death or the opening of the will. The basic differences between the common law and civil law regulation of estates existed in 1850 as they do today. The exclusive applicability of either Swiss or American law was therefore modified in article V, paragraph 1 of the treaty by the proviso that "in the absence of such heir, heirs or other successors, the same care shall be taken by the authorities for the preservation of the property that would be taken for the preservation of the property of a native of the same country, until the lawful proprietor shall have had time to take measures for possessing himself of the same." This provision means that American courts, should Swiss law apply, can appoint an administrator only if the lawful successor cannot take care of his interests personally or through an attorney; that the administrator must yield at any time to the successor or to the Swiss administrator; and that the objective of the administration is the "preservation of the property" rather than the protection of the creditors. Consequently, as a rule there should be no administration (important from the viewpoint of costs), and if ordered, the administration should be conducted differently from a typical one or even from an ancillary one, this difference to be defined by the letters of administration. To the extent that administration is barred by the treaty, creditors of the decedent may protect themselves by garnishment of his assets.

The principle of "universal succession" has been directly recognized

---

[124] ZGB art. 560.
[125] *Id.* art. 594.

by American courts in conflict cases involving French contacts,[126] but its application to Swiss situations by New York surrogates' courts has not been satisfactory. In cases involving personal property left in New York by a Swiss decedent, the court, while admitting the control of Swiss law over the succession, appointed administrators for the protection of New York creditors.[127] The treaty was nowhere mentioned; apparently, here again, it was overlooked by all concerned. As pointed out, the treaty permits public administration if solely for the purpose of preserving the property of the foreign heir, and then only until the latter can himself take possession of the property.

The Swiss Federal Tribunal has shown a very liberal attitude regarding the administration of estates. A Swiss woman who died in Chicago, her last domicile, left personal property in Switzerland. The administrator appointed by the Chicago surrogate brought suit in Switzerland for the property. The Federal Tribunal recognized not only Illinois jurisdiction over the estate, but also the administrator's power to sue in Switzerland, though the letters of administration were couched in terms limited to the Illinois territory.[128] True, under the treaty the Chicago surrogate would have been justified in extending the administrator's power to Swiss territory, but this was not done and there is no indication that the surrogate knew of the treaty. The merits of the claim were not dealt with by the Federal Tribunal.[129]

G. Corporations and Other Organizations

The Treaty of 1850 is concerned with the rights of "citizens" and of governments. The question whether corporations are "citizens" within the purview of the treaty arose when the National Industrial Recovery Act of 1933 imposed an excise tax of five per cent on certain dividends received by foreign corporations.[130] After Swiss insurance companies were assessed for this tax, the Swiss government protested on the ground that, according to article II, paragraph 2 of the treaty,[131]

---

[126] Anglo-California Nat. Bank v. Lazard, 106 F. 2d 693, 698 (9th Cir. 1939); Roques v. Grosjean, 66 N.Y.S. 2d 348 (Sup. Ct. 1946) [French heir "the sole legateee"].

[127] Matter of Barandon, 41 Misc. 380, 84 N.Y. Supp. 937 (Surr. Ct. 1903) [an American postlude to the Feldis case, *supra* note 94]; Matter of Batsholts, *supra* note 116.

[128] Nussle v. Ros, *supra* note 117. Still, the *Restatement of the Law of Conflict of Laws* (1934), §507 provides: "In the absence of a statute permitting it, a foreign administrator cannot sue to recover a claim belonging to the decedent."

[129] Still less is the surrogate entitled, under the treaty, to determine the distribution of the estate as was done in Matter of Lullin, *supra* note 115, referring to a Swiss citizen who had died in Switzerland. Her domicile was not indicated. The court referred to ZGB arts. 457, 462, 473, 733, 750 and 767.

[130] Sec. 213(a), 48 Stat. 195.

[131] *Infra* page 44.

no higher impost must be exacted from Swiss "citizens" than from Americans. The American government, upholding the excise tax, pointed out that the term "citizen" as used in the treaty envisaged natural persons only, and in this interpretation the Swiss government acquiesced.[132]

However, the absence of specific treaty provisions does not matter very much. Even under treaties, foreign corporations are not considered "citizens,"[133] a concept reserved for natural persons in American[134] as well as in Swiss law.[135] Nor is this question of great importance. The main legal problem for a foreign corporation is to do work in the United States, and vice versa. In the United States, the solution has to be found primarily in the law of the particular state envisaged by the foreign corporation for its work; treaty provisions have little effect in this respect. For the foreign corporation (or for foreign non-corporate enterprises) it may appear desirable to establish in the American state, say in New York, a subsidiary corporation. Here, certain restrictions must be considered which, however, are not very severe. Under New York law, for instance, two-thirds of the incorporators (though not of the financiers) and at least one of the directors must be United States citizens, and at least one incorporator and the American director must reside in New York State as well.[136] The regulation in Pennsylvania (with respect to incorporators, but not directors) is very similar,[137] whereas in California no such restrictions exist.[138]

However, a Swiss or other foreign [139] corporation, without creating a subsidiary corporation, may establish a branch or appoint an agent to "do business" in the State of New York, but such action requires a certificate of authority obtainable from the New York Secretary

---

132 3 Hackworth, *op. cit. supra* note 26, at 431.

133 See, *e.g.*, Hawkins, *op. cit. supra* note 22, at 3; Walker, "Provisions on Companies in United States Commercial Treaties", 50 Am. J. Int'l L. 373 (1956).

134 Leaving aside insignificant peculiarities of state law. See, *e.g.*, R. S. Stevens, *Handbook on the Law of Private Corporations* (2d ed. 1949), 36, 52; 18 W. M. Fletcher, *Cyclopedia of the Law of Private Corporations* (1955), §606.

135 Fleiner and Giacometti, *op. cit. supra* note 31, ch. 3, regarding federal and cantonal citizenship (*Bürgerrecht*). However, with regard to some particular questions such as freedom of trade, the position of citizens is not denied to Swiss corporations. *Id.* at 284, n. 3.

136 General Corporation Law §§7 and 27.

137 Purdon's Pa. Stat. Ann., tit. 15, §2852-201, dealing with "business" corporations. *Cf. id.* §2852-401.

138 Cal. Corporations Code (West's Ann. Cal. Codes, vol. 24) §§300-301.

139 Corporations established in another member state of the Union are likewise "foreign" and, of course, constitute the overwhelming majority of "foreign" corporations. On corporations established outside the United States, *cf.* Drachsler, "The Status of Alien Corporations", 23 Fordham L. Rev. 49 (1954), which is not concerned with the particular American-Swiss situation.

of State under certain formal requirements.[140] "Doing business" without such authority renders its contracts entered into within the state unenforceable,[141] but this rule does not cover "incidental business," a concept which is liberally interpreted.[142] Also, a foreign corporation may bring a suit in the New York courts and may be sued there even if not "doing business" in the technical sense.[143] The Pennsylvania law is stricter.[144] In California it is particularly easy to obtain the license for doing business within the state,[145] but an unlicensed corporation cannot bring an action on "intrastate business."[146]

In Switzerland, corporation law is exclusively federal[147] and far clearer, though by no means simple. Contrary to American practice, bearer shares predominate, and privileged-voting shares (*Stimmrechtsactien*) are widely used.[148] (Nevertheless, as mentioned above, there is no public institution like the American Securities and Exchange Commission to protect the financial interests of the public at large.)

Swiss law does not require that the incorporators have Swiss citizenship or Swiss residence. However, the majority of the directors must meet both requirements[149]—a protection of the national interest more effective than the pertinent provisions of the American states. On the other hand, a foreign corporation or other firm need not turn to the government in order to establish a branch in Switzerland. No more is required than the appointment of a Swiss agent and the registration at the commercial register provided by the canton according to the federal law;[150] local jurisdiction over the corporation with

---

140 N. Y. General Corporation Law §210.

141 *Id.* §218.

142 22 McKinney's Consolidated Laws, annotation to §218, n. 34.

143 N. Y. General Corporation Law §§223-225.

Suits against an unlicensed foreign corporation have generally been admitted if the contact with the state is sufficient to render the exercise of jurisdiction reasonable. International Shoe Co. v. State of Washington, 326 U.S. 310 (1945); McGee v. International Life Insurance Co., 355 U.S. 220 (1957).

144 To transact business without qualifying is a misdemeanor, and renders contracts made within the state unenforceable. Purdon's Pa. Stat. Ann., tit. 15, §3144, and annotation to §3142.

145 *Cf.* H. W. Ballantine and G. L. Sterling, *California Corporation Laws* (1949), ch. 18, §403.

146 *Cf.* Cal. Corporations Code (West's Ann. Cal. Codes, vol. 24) §6801, a restriction also recognized where suit is brought in a federal court. Woods v. Interstate Realty Co., 337 U.S. 535 (1949). Nevertheless, suit may be brought in California *against* such a corporation. American de Forest Wireless Telegraph Co. v. Superior Court, 155 Cal. 533, 76 Pac. 15 (1908).

147 OR arts. 620-763.

148 *Cf.* Schmid, "Corporate Control in Switzerland", 6 Am. J. Comp. L. 27 (1957).

149 OR art. 711.

150 *Id.* art. 935, par. 2.

respect to transactions of the branch is thereby created.[151] Even if such a branch is not established, the foreign corporation may sue or be sued in Switzerland;[152] the competence of the court depends on cantonal law. Jurisdiction does not depend on service of process in Switzerland, but primarily on the domicile of the defendant and in part also on other grounds (*e.g.*, place of contracting, place of performance of a contract, place where a tort has been committed).[153]

A peculiar, almost unique, rule of Swiss law permits the "immigration" of a foreign corporation—*i.e.*, its complete transfer without loss of its legal status or identity. Consent of the Federal Council, the executive branch of the Swiss government, is required.[154] The rule is aimed primarily at foreign holding-companies, because of the Swiss policy of facilitating the influx of foreign capital.

Under modern conditions, problems may arise where a corporation adopts the name of a foreign corporation. In *Interchemical Corporation v. Interchemie A.-G.*, the Swiss Federal Tribunal took the view that the American corporation involved would not be protected since it was doing no business in Switzerland worth mentioning.[155] Under American law, a corporation will generally be protected against the use of its name, such use being considered a kind of unfair competition,[156] but there are no cases in point concerned with corporations of Switzerland or other civil law countries.

American-Swiss relations in the field of corporation law have been somewhat disturbed by the contrast in their respectively belligerent and neutral attitudes during and after World War II. This contrast has been emphasized by the peculiar Swiss banking law designed to offer the highest degree of secrecy to foreign banking customers. Under article 47 of the federal law on banks and savings banks (*Banken und Sparkassen*) of November 8, 1934, punishment up to 20,000 francs or imprisonment up to six months is inflicted upon a person working for a bank and wilfully infringing its "professional secrecy."[157] In addition, article 273 of the Federal Criminal Code (*Strafgesetzbuch*) of December 21, 1937 imposes imprisonment—in grave cases, in a penitentiary (*Zuchthaus*)—upon those who render accessible a matter of business secrecy (*Geschäftsgeheimnis*) to a foreign organism, official or private, or to a foreign private enterprise or agent thereof.[158] This extreme penalty for the surrender of *private*

---

[151] *Id.* art. 642, par. 3.
[152] Julliard v. Havana Commercial Company, BGE 35(II) 451, 458 (1909).
[153] See *infra* page 47.
[154] OR Transitional Provisions (*Schluss- und Übergangsbestimmungen*) art. 14.
[155] BGE 79(II) 305 (1953).
[156] Stevens, *op. cit. supra* note 134, at 130.
[157] AS 51, 117; BS 10, 337.
[158] AS 54, 757; BS 3, 203.

business secrets to any foreigner (or to a foreign court) is perplexing, but the penal version of the Banking Act is even more efficient, since the banker will be inclined to deny information also in case of doubt. This whole kind of criminal approach is unique and very much in contrast to the American view which not only keeps banking secrecy out of the criminal law, but also submits it, as will be seen, to other limitations.

This difference in the Swiss and American political and legal approaches has been of importance due to the fact that before or during World War II, German investors acquired a considerable number of Swiss shares and gained control of Swiss corporations holding assets in the United States. When confronted with such a case, the American authorities refused to grant the Swiss corporation the privilege of neutrality, and the corporate assets were subject to seizure as enemy property under the Trading with the Enemy Act of October 6, 1917.[159] In such a situation, the "corporate veil" must be "pierced"[160] in order to discover the persons actually in control of the enterprise. The outstanding example was the seizure by the American government of the American assets, amounting to more than one hundred million dollars, of the "Société Internationale pour Participations Industrielles et Commerciales S.A.", better known as "Interhandel", on the ground of prima facie evidence indicating German control of that corporation. Thereupon Interhandel brought suit against the government, asserting that its supposition was wrong. The government filed a motion to the effect that plaintiff should produce for judicial inspection, among others, a large number of documents held by a Swiss bank and relating to Interhandel. After the court had granted this order, the Swiss Attorney General seized the documents on the ground that their submission would be punishable under Swiss law as espionage and as a violation of banking secrecy. Thereupon the court rejected the suit because Interhandel had not furnished the evidence required under American law, which was

---

[159] 40 Stat. 411, 55 Stat. 839, 50 U.S.C. Appendix §§1-39 (1952; supp. V, 1958). Under the Swiss-Allied Accord of May 25, 1946, 14 Dept. State Bull. 1121 (1946), half of the German assets in Switzerland were to go to the Allies and the other half to Switzerland, but finally the total assets were left to Switzerland by the Swiss-Allied Agreement of August 28, 1952, 27 Dept. State Bull. 363 (1952), AS 1953, 131, in exchange for a payment of 121,500,000 francs, a sum which Switzerland was authorized by Western Germany to take from certain German assets. AS 1953, 117.

[160] Domke, " 'Piercing the Corporate Veil' in the Law of Economic Warfare", 1955 Wis. L. Rev. 77; Timberg, "The Corporation as a Technique of International Administration", 19 U. Chi. L. Rev. 739 (1952). [The customary phraseology originated with Maurice Wormser, "Piercing the Veil of Corporate Entity", 12 Colum. L. Bev. 496 (1912).]

considered governing as a matter of procedure.[161] The elaborate and careful decision, which did not question the lawfulness and integrity of the action taken by the Attorney General under Swiss law, was affirmed by the Court of Appeals;[162] a review was twice declined by the Supreme Court which, however, later reversed on procedural grounds.[163] Earlier, when American stockholders of Interhandel had claimed a right to the corporate assets proporionate to their stock, the Supreme Court granted the claim.[164] It took the same position in favor of a Lichtenstein citizen residing in the United States, who owned shares of another Swiss corporation controlled by Germans.[165] There is no doubt that according to this doctrine Swiss citizens, if "innocent" shareholders of such a corporation, would be entitled to the protection of their proportionate interests. Still, so far, the distribution of proportionate assets to the "innocents" seems to have encountered calculative and other difficulties which have not yet been overcome. The apportionment proclaimed by the Supreme Court is of an ambiguous character and was impressively opposed by a strong minority of the Court (three against five judges).

The *Interhandel* case has aroused worldwide attention particularly because the Swiss government has asked the United States government to submit the final decision to arbitration or conciliation on the basis of the Swiss-American Treaty of February 16, 1931 on Arbitration and Conciliation[166] as well as of the Swiss-Allied Accord of May 25, 1946.[167] The American government has declined submission. This problem, now confronting the International Court of Justice at The Hague, stands outside the scope of this study.[168]

---

[161] Société Internationale v. McGranery, 111 F. Supp. 435 (D. D.C. 1953).

[162] 225 F. 2d 532 (App. D.C. 1955).

[163] Certiorari was denied, 350 U.S. 937 (1956) and a rehearing denied, 350 U.S. 976 (1956). However, the Supreme Court later granted certiorari, 355 U.S. 812 (1957) and then remanded merely on the ground that rule 37, F. R. Civ. P., 28 U.S.C.A., "should not be construed to authorize dismissal of this complaint because of petitioner's noncompliance with a pretrial production order when it has been established that failure to comply has been due to inability, and not to willfulness, bad faith, or any fault of petitioner". 357 U.S. 197, 212 (1958).

[164] Kaufman v. Société Internationale, 343 U.S. 156 (1952).

[165] Clark v. Uebersee Finanz-Korporation, 332 U.S. 480 (1947). Compare Uebersee Finanz-Korporation v. McGrath, 343 U.S. 205 (1952).

[166] TS 847; AS 48, 290; BS 11, 381.

[167] 14 Dept. State Bull. 1121 (1946).

[168] See Interhandel Case (interim measures of protection), Order of October 24th, 1957: I.C.J. Reports 1957, p. 105.

The problem has been discussed by Briggs — the result being in favor of Switzerland — in "Towards the Rule of Law?", 51 Am. J. Int'l L. 517 (1957).

Swiss experiences during World War II and the post-War period have caused the Swiss Federal Council to provide certain precautionary measures for "interna-

Apart from the effects of the war, the extreme Swiss secrecy in banking matters had caused disturbances in the American protection of holders of corporate assets under the Securities Exchange Act of 1934[169] and under the controlling measures of the Securities and Exchange Commission,[170] both important parts of the New Deal legislation. For instance, under the Securities Exchange Act, persons owning directly or indirectly more than ten per cent of a definite security type have to file reports; the same rule applies to any officer of the issuer of such a security. Furthermore, the "proxy" rules of the commission[171] require, in connection with the election of directors, exact statements on the pertinent securities held by directors and nominees, and further detailed information in case of a contest for the election. In these and other matters, the Swiss attitude is an important factor. The value of American stock held by Swiss residents was estimated at 1,353 million dollars by the end of 1954, and 1,796 million by the end of 1955; and Swiss net purchases in American securities amounted in 1956 to 118 million dollars—that is, nearly half the total purchases from foreign countries.[172] Obviously, the strict secrecy required by Swiss law means a serious weakening of the American system, the value of which can hardly be denied, and negotiations to improve the situation have been opened between the two governments.[173]

As is well known, the trust, in contrast to the corporation, represents a phenomenon peculiar to the common law. Its growing effect-

---

tional conflicts" (not necessarily wars) of the future. Temporary transfer of registered branches of Swiss commercial firms has been permitted in case of such emergencies by a decree of the Federal Council of April 12, 1957, AS 1957, 337. A decree of the same date, AS 1957, 354, grants the firms various protective measures such as cancellation of certain securities they have issued. Governmental approval is not required for the application of these decrees.

[169] 48 Stat. 881, 15 U.S.C. §§78a-78jj (1952).

[170] *Cf.* especially hearings of the United States Senate, 85th Cong., 1st Sess.: (a) Subcommittee of Committee on Banking and Currency, *SEC Enforcement Problems*, pt. I, 41, 53-54, 161-163 (Mar. 5, 1957); (b) Subcommittee of Committee on the Judiciary, *Scope of Soviet Activity in the United States*, pt. 59, 3829, 3835, 3897 (Apr. 9-10, 1957); at pp. 3829-3844, the Chairman of the SEC, Mr. Armstrong, offers a most instructive survey, emphasizing the "serious problems for the Commission" created by Swiss institutions and attitudes.

[171] SEC, *Proxy Rules* (1956).

[172] See Hearings of Subcommittee of Committee on Banking and Currency, *supra* note 170, at 53 and 161; Hearings of Subcommittee of Committee on the Judiciary, *supra* note 170, at 3835.

[173] Hearings of Subcommittee of Committee on the Judiciary, *supra* note 170, at 3897. It has been pointed out by Swiss delegates, and admitted by American members of the Committee, that the Swiss secrecy rules had their genesis in the rise of Fascism and similar political developments, but it may be added that adaptation to changed circumstances appears desirable.

iveness in the economic field has attracted the attention of jurists in all civil law countries, including Switzerland. The trust has not only been the subject of several Swiss studies,[174] but the Swiss Lawyers' Association initiated an extensive and careful discussion of whether the trust should be introduced into the Swiss legal system.[175] The answer was negative, as in nearly all[176] civil law countries.

This, of course, does not mean that a Swiss court would deny the validity of an American trust or deny the right of the trustee to bring a suit on its behalf in Switzerland. There is no case in point,[177] but the liberal attitude of Swiss courts toward foreign institutions leaves little doubt as to what the outcome of such a case would be. Even if, for one reason or another (say taxation), a common law trust had been signed in Switzerland the agreement would hardly be held invalid though the legal effects of the trust on Swiss assets might be obscure.

Strangely enough, in contrast to the absence of pertinent Swiss cases, American courts have been preoccupied repeatedly with the Swiss *Familienstiftung*,[178] an institution somewhat similar to the common law family trust and apparently attractive to foreign capitalists for taxation or other reasons. American assets of two *Familienstiftungen* have been the subject of litigation following the death of the respective settlors. In each case the *Familienstiftung* was convincingly held invalid for lack of the Swiss statutory prerequisites—an indication of a spurious approach to the Swiss institution. While one of the cases resulted only in a brief decision,[179] the other led to

---

174 F. Weiser, *Trusts on the Continent of Europe* (1936) is still outstanding. See also Meyer, "Trusts and Swiss Law", 1 Int'l & Comp. L. Q. 378 (1952); Bloch, "Der anglo-amerikanische Trust und seine Behandlung im internationalen Privatrecht", SJZ 46, 65 (1950); B. Hugi, *Der Amerikanische Investment Trust* (thesis Bern 1936), which gives details on Swiss investment in American securities; and the studies referred to *infra* note 175.

175 See Reymond, "Le Trust et le droit suisse", ZSR 73, 121a (1954); Gubler, "Besteht in der Schweiz ein Bedürfnis nach der Einführung des Instituts der angelsächsischen Treuhand (trust)?", *id.* at 215a; [Protocol of the General Assembly of the Swiss Lawyers' Association], *id.* at 477a.

176 In addition to Lichtenstein, Mexico and Panama are exceptions, though the legal structure of the trust is there somewhat obscure. A general discussion is offered by Hefti, "Trusts and Their Treatment in the Civil Law", 5 Am. J. Comp. L. 553 (1956).

177 The cases Böckli v. Konkursmasse Nachlass Mayer, BGE 78(II) 445 (1952) and Aktiebolaget Obligationsinteressenter v. Bank für Internationalen Zahlungsangleich, BGE 62(II) 140 (1936) are merely concernd with *Treuhand*, a German-Swiss concept, inspired by the trust, but the approach of the court supports the presumption that a favorable attitude would be taken toward the trust.

178 ZGB art. 335; see Bloch, "Die Ungültigkeit von Familienstiftungen und ihre rechtlichen Folgen", SJZ 53, 1 (1957); Domke, "Schweizer Interessen vor amerikanischen Gerichten", SJZ 53, 234 (1957).

179 Estate of von Schertel, N.Y.L.J., Nov. 25, 1949, p. 1377, col. 6 (Surr. Ct.).

two extensive judicial inquiries. A wealthy Indonesian domiciled in the Netherlands had tried to turn part of his property into a *Familienstiftung*, but after his death this transaction was declared invalid by a New York surrogate[180] because the *Familienstiftung* had not been limited to the "education, endowment and assistance in case of need" of family members, as required by the Swiss Code. The same view was taken by the United States Tax Court in a very comprehensive opinion.[181] Both courts followed the opinions of Swiss legal experts.

*　　*　　*　　*　　*

The contrast between American and Swiss law is perhaps even more striking within the sphere of the so-called anti-trust law. This law operates against restraint of trade caused by monopolistic or similar conspiratorial arrangements which endanger the free and competitive market considered necessary for the consumers, the working class, and the general structure of the business community.[182] Arrangements of this type are usually trusts or have trust-like features. In the United States this "anti-trust" feeling is particularly strong. Suits may be brought against the enterprises even by the federal government itself.[183] In Switzerland, too, an anti-trust movement has recently developed; still, in January 1958 a legislative measure against Swiss cartels was rejected by a strong majority in a plebiscite, apparently because of defects of the project. Yet the American anti-trust law is noteworthy for Switzerland because, under modern conditions, monopolistic arrangements include an increasing number of

---

[180] Estate of Oei Tjong Swan, 152 N.Y.S. 2d 225 [fuller text in N.Y.L.J., Apr. 6, 1956, p. 8, col. 2] (Surr. Ct.), *aff'd*, 156 N.Y.S. 2d 1009 (App. Div., 1st Dep't, 1956) — ordering restitution of New York property conferred as part of the *Familienstiftung*.

[181] Estate of Oei Tjong Swan, 24 T.C. 829 (1955), *rev'd on other grounds* [relating to the United States tax law], 247 F. 2d 144 (2d Cir. 1957).

[182] *Cf.* W. Friedmann, *Anti-Trust Laws: A Comparative Symposium* (1956). Pt. I analyzes the national laws, especially that of the United States (by Timberg, at 403-466); pt. II deals with international cartels and combines (by Friedmann and van Themaat, at 469-515); pt. III presents a comparative analysis (by Friedmann, at 519-558). The Swiss situation is not included in this symposium. Extensive studies on the American system are also offered by the United States Congress, Senate Committee on the Judiciary, *A Study of the Antitrust Laws* (6 vols. 1955-1956); by H. A. Toulmin, *A Treatise on the Anti-Trust Laws of the United States and Including all Related Trade Regulatory Laws* (7 vols. 1949-1952); and by the American Bar Association, Section of Antitrust Law, *An Antitrust Handbook* (1958) [especially Timberg, "Problems of International Business", at 49-63]. There are also some valuable Swiss studies on this subject, especially E. Curti, *Das Antitrustrecht der Vereinigten Staaten von Amerika* (1955). *Cf.* also F. Petitpierre, *L'Application du droit antitrust des Etats-Unis d'Amérique à leur commerce extérieur* (1956) and H. H. Jenny, *Die Amerikanischen Antitrust-Gesetze* (thesis Bern 1952).

[183] Law of July 2, 1890 ("Sherman Act"), §4, 26 Stat. 209, 15 U.S.C. §4 (1952).

international elements; and because Switzerland, due to her international neutrality, her financial stability and her favorable attitude toward foreign funds, has made herself attractive in this field as well.

In this connection, it may be mentioned that the United States government brought a suit against several Swiss and American corporations, alleging that an American watch-producing company (Longines) owned all the shares of a Swiss firm (Wittnauer) and had concluded with it a "collective convention" to "prevent the free manufacture, sale and export by others of Swiss and American watches and watch parts." No judgment was rendered on the substance of the case, but the federal court stated its jurisdiction over the matter with convincing arguments.[184]

The facts underlying this case are unusual and certainly do not constitute a threat to Swiss business. Nevertheless, conditions render it desirable for Swiss enterprises to be careful in entering into arrangements which might cause a restraint of trade affecting the American market; the restrictions prescribed by American law, though not very stringent, should certainly be examined under such circumstances.

H. *Conventions on Copyright, Patent and Trade Mark*

The United States and Switzerland are both members of two widespread international conventions: the Universal Copyright Convention of 1952,[185] and the multipartite Convention for the Protection of Industrial Property of 1934 (the latter dealing with patents as well as trade marks).[186] These conventions are implemented by national statutes; the Universal Copyright Convention by its own terms is to be carried out by means of domestic legislation.

---

[184] United States v. The Watchmakers of Switzerland Information Center, 134 F. Supp. 710 (S.D.N.Y. 1955). In United States v. Aluminum Co. of America, 148 F. 2d 416 (2d Cir. 1945), the much-discussed "Alcoa" case, a Canadian corporation controlled by a United States corporation had entered into a cartel agreement with a Swiss and certain other European corporations. Under this agreement, a Swiss corporation founded by the signatories was to be the chief manager of the cartel. The agreement was declared invalid in an extensive opinion written by Judge Learned Hand.

[185] Joined by the United States in 1954, TIAS 3324, and by Switzerland in 1955, AS 1956, 101; 9 Unesco Copyright Bulletin 129 (1956). *Cf.* Unesco, *Copyright Laws and Treaties of the World* (loose-leaf, 1956); T. R. Kupferman and M. Foner, *Universal Copyright Convention Analyzed* (1955); Sherman, "The Universal Copyright Convention: Its Effect on United States Law", 55 Colum. L. Rev. 1137 (1955); Schulman, "International Copyright in the United States: A Critical Analysis", 19 Law & Contemp. Prob. 141 (1954).

[186] 192 LNTS 17. Adhered to by Switzerland in 1929, AS 45, 243; BS 11, 977; by the United States in 1938, 53 Stat. 1748, TS 941.

The basis of American copyright is the Act of July 30, 1947,[187] which has been adapted to the international convention by the Act of August 31, 1954.[188] Under these regulations, the copyright requires, in a rather complicated way (sections 6 and 7), a registration of the book or other admissible work (*e.g.*, photograph) at the Copyright Office in Washington; the copyright lasts twenty-eight years from the date of the first publication, a period which may be extended for another twenty-eight years upon application by the holder. The so-called "manufacturing clause" (section 16) provides a somewhat perplexing condition for obtaining a copyright: any book written in English by a citizen or domiciliary of the United States must be printed in this country—a prerequisite introduced in 1891 on demand of the printing-trade unions because of the considerably lower wage rates in many foreign countries. The import into the United States of English-language books not printed in accordance with this clause (for instance, printed in Switzerland) is forbidden, but under the 1954 Act an exemption is granted for fifteen hundred copies. On the basis of a simple American registration, these copies receive a temporary copyright for five years, which may be made definitive for twenty-eight years if a new edition is published in the United States in accordance with the manufacturing clause during that five-year period.

Swiss law[189] has no such manufacturing clause, and no registration or other formality is required for the establishment of the copyright, which extends for fifty years following the author's death. As a result of the international convention, American citizens may obtain Swiss copyrights under Swiss law, and Swiss citizens may obtain American copyrights under American law. (If not residents of the United States, the latter are not affected by the manufacturing clause.) As a general rule, any copyright acquired under Swiss law will be recognized in the United States and vice versa, provided the work bears the letter C enclosed within a circle, accompaneid by the name of the author or other "copyright proprietor" and the year of the first publication. Nevertheless, English-language works by American citizens or domiciliaries remain restricted by the manufacturing clause.

The Convention for the Protection of Industrial Property provides that if a patent application is filed in one member country, such as the United States, it will be considered to have the same filing date in every other member country—for example, Switzerland—if another

---

[187] 61 Stat. 652. The text and its numerous amendments are found in tit. 17 of the United States Code (1952 ed.).

[188] 68 Stat. 1030. See also Lüdi, "Einige internationale Aspekte des Urheberrechts in den Vereinigten Staaten", SJZ 51, 85 (1955).

[189] Statutes of December 7, 1922, AS 39, 65; BS 2, 817; of September 25, 1940, AS 57, 117; BS 2, 834; and of June 24, 1955, AS 1955, 855.

application is filed there within twelve months. Hence the inventor will also be protected in Switzerland against a patent application made by another person for the same invention after the day of the American application. Also, an American citizen may first submit his application in Switzerland, or a Swiss citizen may do so in the United States. Regarding trade marks, under the convention priority is preserved in the other country for six months following the date when the first application was filed.

Basically, the law of patents and trade marks is domestic in both countries. In the United States[190] a patent can be granted only to a natural person, the inventor; in Switzerland it may also be granted to a corporation. The patent expires in the United States after seventeen years, and in Switzerland after eighteen years. Protection of trade marks expires in either country after twenty years, but on application this period may be extended.

In Switzerland the legislature has transferred a considerable discretion to the Federal Council (*Bundesrat*), thereby rendering the regulations more flexible.[191] American patent law is more complex than the Swiss system, and is found in case law to a larger extent. Thus American courts have applied the anti-trust concept to situations where the arrangements between patentees and licensees involved too broad a suppression of competition,[192] an approach unknown to Swiss law.

I. Tax Conventions

In the United States and Switzerland, taxation is complicated by the fact that even in the fundamental matter of personal income, each federal government and its member states or cantons has power to collect taxes separately. However, the management of taxation differs greatly: in Switzerland the emphasis is on cantonal laws, especially as regards the income tax; a federal income tax (called *Wehrsteuer*) amounts to a mere fraction of the cantonal income taxes.[193]

---

[190] Patent Act of July 19, 1952, 66 Stat. 792, tit. 35, U.S.C. (1952).

[191] Patent Law of June 25, 1954, AS 1955, 871. See A. Reimer, *Schweizerische Gesetzgebung zum Gewerblichen Rechtsschutz* (1956). A comprehensive inquiry has been started by R. Blum and M. M. Pedrazzini, *Das Schweizerische Patentrecht* (vol. 1, 1957).

[192] L. I. Wood, *Patents and Antitrust Law* (1942); 4 Toulmin, *op. cit. supra* note 182.

[193] A survey of Swiss tax law is offered in W. J. Gibbons, *Tax Factors in Basing International Business Abroad* (1957), 133 ff.; however, it gives the misleading impression that the federal income tax (*Wehrsteuer*) is imposed only on corporations, while in fact it is also exacted from natural persons. Federal Council, Order of December 9, 1940, AS 56, 1947; BS 6, 350.

The Treaty of 1850 (article II, paragraph 2) provides only that no higher impost shall be exacted from the citizens of one of the two countries, residing or established in the other, than shall be levied upon citizens of the country in which they reside. This is an elaboration of the last sentence of article I, paragraph 1 of the treaty, under which no "pecuniary or other more burdensome condition", not imposed upon citizens, shall be imposed "upon their residence or establishment." When California enacted an alien poll tax law in 1921 and the Swiss government protested, the United States government recognized that article II, paragraph 2 of the treaty had been violated by California.[194] Actually the Supreme Court of California soon declared the whole act unconstitutional.[195]

The situation has now been improved by the American-Swiss Convention of May 24, 1951 on the Avoidance of Double Taxation with Respect to Taxes on Income.[196] The basic provision of this convention exempts Swiss enterprises from United States income taxation, and vice versa, unless the enterprise has a "permanent establishment" in the other country. However, carrying on business through a commission agent, a broker, a custodian or other independent agent does not constitute a "permanent establishment." Subsidiary corporations are not affected by the treaty at all, but they are under no danger of double taxation. Individual residents of one of the two countries, working in the other for no more than 183 days, need not pay income taxes there if the compensation received does not exceed $10,000 or if it is duly paid by a person or enterprise of the home country.[197] Especially favorable conditions are provided for teachers and students of one country visiting the other for teaching or studying purposes, respectively.[198]

---

[194] Burckhardt, op. cit. supra note 23, at §1861.

[195] In re Kotta, 187 Cal. 27, 200 Pac. 957 (1921). Erroneously, the Swiss authorities took the view that the judgment was based on the assumption of a treaty violation; see Burckhardt, loc. cit. supra note 194.

[196] 2 UST 1751; TIAS 2316; 127 UNTS 227; AS 1951, 892. Set forth in appendix II, infra pages 65-73. See M. B. Carroll and K. Locher, The Tax Conventions Between the Swiss Confederation and the United States (1951); K. Locher, Handbuch der schweizerisch-amerikanischen Doppelsbesteuerungsabkommen, Einkommens- und Erbschaftssteueren (loose-leaf, 1951-[1957]); both of which also cover the treaty cited infra note 199.

[197] In Legerlotz v. Wehrsteuer-Rekurskommission des Kantons Zürich, BGE 82(I) 1 (1956), the treaty was rightly held inapplicable in the case of an American domiciliary who asked for a reduction of income tax with respect to receipts from Swiss real property.

[198] An interesting decision, not related to the treaty, was rendered by the United States Court of Claims in Karrer v. United States, 152 F. Supp. 66 (1957). A Swiss scholar residing in Switzerland and collaborating with a Swiss corporation in the exploitation of an invention of his, had received from an American corporation, with which the Swiss corporation had contracted, payments

A Convention on the Avoidance of Double Taxation with Respect to Taxes on Estates and Inheritances was concluded between the two countries on July 9, 1951.[199] Confronted with considerable legal difficulties, this complicated convention has but limited significance. It rules mainly that the American part of the estates of persons who were citizens or residents of Switzerland at the time of their death will be granted the tax allowance usually reserved to estates of United States domiciliaries (a tax-free amount of $60,000); a similar exemption is granted by Switzerland to estates of Americans domiciled there. The convention is also concerned with American-Swiss dual citizenship; if both governments consider the decedent as having been their citizen or domiciliary, a complex tax reduction goes into effect.

A certain flaw of the conventions consists in the fact that on the American side they do not affect the states, most of which also impose income as well as inheritance taxes. This gap does not involve much danger, however, for contrary to Swiss cantonal taxes, the pertinent American states taxes are relatively low. This is shown by the following figures, presenting (in thousands of dollars): (a) state income tax collections and (b) federal income tax collections in California, New York and Pennsylvania,[200] for the year 1955.[201]

	a. STATE		*b. FEDERAL*	
	Indiv.	*Corp.*	*Indiv.*	*Corp.*
California	106,557	133,412	2,931,650	1,101,537
New York	367,466	207,215	5,482,896	4,748,942
Pennsylvania		97,911	2,265,694	1,191,339

No similar figures comparing federal and state estate taxes are available, but in this respect a basic relief is afforded by the fact that within certain limits the state estate tax can be deducted from the federal estate tax.[202]

Questions of taxation may become relevant also in the interpretation of wills. This happened when a New York surrogate had to define an "annual income" granted to a Swiss resident by testament. The court

---

for which he had paid more than $200,000 in income taxes to the United States government. The court held that he was under no obligation to pay an income tax, and the government was required to refund the whole amount.

199 3 UST 3972; TIAS 2533; 165 UNTS 51; AS 1952, 645. Set forth in appendix III, *infra* pages 75-78. For explanation, see the writings cited *supra* note 196.

200 Pennsylvania has an income tax only for corporations.

201 I am indebted for these figures to Mr. Charles E. Brush, Director of Field Research, Tax Foundation, New York City.

202 26 U.S.C. §2011 (1952; supp. V, 1958).

interpreted the will to mean that the thirty per cent tax due for such income must be paid by the trustee without deducting it from the amount to be paid to the Swiss legatee.[203]

---

[203] *In re* Mansbendel's Estate, 145 N.Y.S. 2d 807 (Surr. Ct. 1955).

Chapter II

MATTERS OF CIVIL PROCEDURE

A. *International Jurisdiction of Courts*

Swiss courts and laws of procedure are mainly cantonal; the Federal Tribunal functions under the constitution and under the federal laws as a supreme court of review over the decisions of the cantonal courts.[204] In addition to the federal law, the procedural laws of the cantons of Basel-City,[205] Bern,[206] Geneva,[207] and Zürich,[208] will be considered here.

Regarding the jurisdiction of courts, some fundamental differences between American and civil law principles[209] (which dominate Swiss law) must be kept in mind. Under civil law, service of process upon a person is not constitutive of jurisdiction in personam as it is under Anglo-American law.[210] Jurisdiction in personam is created by such

---

[204] The leading works in this field are two books by M. Guldener, *Das Schweizerische Zivilprozessrecht* (2 vols. 1947-1948) (cited hereafter as Guldener, *Schw. Z.P.R.*) and *Das Internationale und Interkantonale Zivilprozessrecht der Schweiz* (1951) (cited hereafter as Guldener, *Int. Z.P.R.*). A valuable comparative inquiry into a basic problem is presented by Schoch in "Conflict of Laws in a Federal State: The Experience of Switzerland", 55 Harv. L. Rev. 738, 756 *ff.* (1942).

[205] Code of Civil Procedure (*Zivilprozessordnung*) of February 8, 1875, *Gesamtausgabe der Basler Gesetzessammlung* (1913), 225, as amended; *cf. Gesamtausgabe der Basler Gesetzessammlung bis* 1929 (1939), 140 (cited hereafter as *Basel*).

[206] *Zivilprozessordnung* of July 7, 1918 [in G. Leuch, *Die Zivilprozessordnung für den Kanton Bern* (1937)] (cited hereafter as *Bern*).

[207] *Loi sur l'organisation judiciaire* of Nov. 22, 1941, *Recueil des Lois* 127, 144 (Geneva 1941), as amended (cited hereafter as *Geneva Org. Jud.*); furthermore, *Loi de Procédure civile* of Oct. 13, 1920, *Recueil des Lois* 106, 782 (Geneva 1920) (cited hereafter as *Geneva Proc. Civ.*).

[208] *Zivilprozessordnung* of Apr. 13, 1913, *Offizielle Sammlung der seit 10. März 1831 erlassenen Gesetze, Beschlüsse und Verordnungen des Eidgenössischen Standes Zürich* 29, 522 (1914), as amended [*cf. Offizielle Sammlung*, vol. 39, *Titelregister*] (cited hereafter as *Zürich*).

[209] See Nussbaum, *op. cit. supra* note 86, at §§20 *ff.*

[210] New York jurisdiction in a suit against a Swiss corporation was established by service of process against a New York agent of the corporation in Varga v. Crédit Suisse, N.Y.L.J. Aug. 3, 1956, p. 3, col. 1 (Sup. Ct.).

factors as (1) domicile,[211] (2) commercial establishment (for transactions connected with the establishment),[212] (3) place of contracting or of performing the contract (for actions arising out of that contract)[213] or (4) committing a tort within the canton (for actions on the tort).[214] Service of process against non-residents may be made in these cases by publication or other forms of constructive service similar to requirements for jurisdiction in rem in the United States. Generally, jurisdiction of Swiss courts over a person residing in the United States cannot be obtained merely by serving process upon that person in Swiss territory. Under Bern law,[215] however, sojourn within the canton is sufficient to give the Bern court jurisdiction in personam over the sojourner, a rule practically identical with that of American law; and under Geneva law, a person neither domiciled nor resident in the canton is subject to Geneva jurisdiction if he has made a contract with a Geneva resident.[216] This provision may warrant Geneva's taking jurisdiction in personam over American citizens personally served with process within the canton.

In American practice, jurisdiction over non-residents is frequently secured by attachment of the alleged debtor's property, with subsequent quasi in rem procedure against the attached property. In Switzerland a similar method is provided by a federal statute of 1889 [217] which makes it possible to attach property of an alleged debtor if he is not domiciled in Switzerland or has no fixed domicile at all. It does not matter whether the creditor is Swiss. He must file the application with the cantonal executive office of the place where

---

[211] *Basel* art. 1, *Bern* art. 20, *Geneva Org. Jud.* art 57(1), *Zürich* art. 1. A Geneva citizen may be sued in Geneva if domiciled or resident in a foreign country different from that of contracting. Piantanida v. Pictet, Cour de justice civile [highest court], Dec. 7, 1917, Semjud 40, 9 (1918). Under art. 59 of the Federal Constitution, a solvent debtor must be sued within the canton of his domicile (*infra* page 49), a provision placing heavy restrictions upon the grounds of cantonal jurisdiction referred to in the text, (2) to (4).

[212] *Basel* art. 1, *Bern* art. 22 (branch establishment), *Zürich* art. 2(6). *Cf.* also OR art. 642(3), 782(3) and 837(3) (branch establishment).

[213] *Basel* art. 3. This applies particularly if the defendant has no settled domicile in Switzerland. *Cf.* Guldener, *Schw. Z.P.R.*, 76.

[214] *Basel* art. 4, *Bern* art. 26.

[215] *Bern* art. 24. The Government Council of the Bern canton has ruled that a Swiss citizen residing in the United States and having property in Switzerland can be sued there for alimony unenforceable under American law. Decree of November 6, 1942, SJZ 39, 184. This theory is questionable.

[216] *Geneva Org. Jud.* art. 57(3). Plaintiff has to prove the reciprocity required. In case the defendant is a Swiss citizen, art. 59 of the Federal Constitution applies. Jandin v. Bartholomaï, Cour de justice civile, Geneva, Mar. 10, 1925, Semjud 47, 374 (1925); *infra* page 49.

[217] Federal law on forced execution and bankruptcy (*Schuldbetreibung und Konkurs*) of April 11, 1889, AS 11, 529, BS 3, 3, art. 271(2) and (4).

the property is situated, and if he offers sufficient prima face evidence, attachment is ordered by the office.[218] Legal controversies concerning the creditor's claim are ordinarily to be solved by the court of the place where the attached property is situated.[219] Bern, following the example of German law, goes further: any suit in personam may be brought in a Bern court against a person not domiciled in Switzerland if the defendant has any property, however little, in the canton.[220] Preliminary attachment is not a prerequisite under this provision. Moreover, the action contemplated by the federal statute of 1889 may be brought for the entire amount of the debt regardless of the lesser value of the attached property, there being under Swiss law no quasi in rem procedure of the American type. While the Swiss judgment would not be recognized in the United States in these cases because rendered by a court without jurisdiction under American principles, there might still be inconveniences for the American party, and he would also be responsible for the fees of the court and of counsel. On the other hand, the requirement that the attaching creditor initiate an ordinary lawsuit within ten days acts to some extent as a check upon ill-considered attachments, as does the obligation to indemnify the debtor where an attachment is found by the court to be unwarranted.[221]

A peculiar aspect of Swiss procedural law is presented by article 59 of the Federal Constitution. Under this provision, a solvent debtor domiciled in Switzerland is entitled to have suits in personam brought against him in the court of his domicile and no other.[222] The rule applies also to non-Swiss citizens[223] and to corporations.[224] In inter-

---

[218] *Id.* arts. 272, 278(2).

[219] *Basel* art. 6; *Bern* art. 25(2); *Geneva Org. Jud.* art. 55; *Zürich* art. 10. The federal law is silent regarding this point of jurisdiction, *cf.* In Sachen Meyer, BGE 40(III) 249 (1914), as well as Navigazione Generale Italiana v. Grandjean & Kons., BGE 57(II) 112 (1931); but the same place of jurisdiction is provided by the federal statute with respect to some specific questions. See Guldener, *Schw. Z.P.R.*, 71. The whole regulation is rather complicated; *cf.* Meyer-Wild, "Zur Frage des Gerichtsstandes für die Arrestprosequierungsklage", SJZ 16, 253 (1920); Hagmann, "Der Gerichtsstand des Arrestortes für die Klage auf Anerkennung de Arrestforderung", SJZ 17, 198 (1921); F. Zuppinger, *Die Arrestprosequierungsklage nach Art. 278 Abs. 2 SchKG* (thesis Zürich 1945).

[220] *Bern* art. 25; German Code of Civil Procedure §23.

[221] Law of April 11, 1889, *supra* note 217, art. 273. An emergency decree of 1939 restricting attachments of the type discussed has been repealed. Decree of the Federal Council of September 3, 1948, AS 1948, 962.

[222] *Cf.* Fleiner and Giacometti, *op. cit. supra* note 31, at 857; Guldener, *Schw. Z.P.R.*, 53.

[223] Espanet v. Sève, BGE 25(I) 89, 92 (1899) (under conditions of art. 59, foreign judgment not executory in Switzerland); Baroni v. Proh & Cie., BGE 52(I) 267 (1926).

[224] Jura-Simplon v. Hayet, BGE 29(I) 299, 303 (1903). The same rule applies to other suable commercial associations, Schweizer Bankverein v. Obergericht Zürich, BGE 53(I) 124 (1937).

national relations, it is particularly important to note that the protection of article 59 may be validly renounced.[225]

In addition to the rules on actions in personam, there are in Swiss law rules establishing the jurisdiction of the *forum rei sitae* over immovables and the jurisdiction of the court of the last domicile over inheritance claims.[226] This conforms to American practice except that under Swiss law the *forum hereditatis* extends also to immovables outside the territory.

Jurisdiction of a court may also be created by an agreement of the parties, and such an accord (*prorogatio*) is more frequent and less restricted in Switzerland,[227] as well as in other civil law countries, than in the United States. In contrast to American practice, Swiss courts may even be "ousted" by such an arrangement.[228] On the other hand, it is possible for a foreigner (*e.g.*, an American) to confer jurisdiction upon a Swiss court by agreement. Under some cantonal laws, however, the courts may use discretion in accepting or declining jurisdiction, at least where both parties are foreign residents.[229]

Whatever the issue of a legal controversy, the parties may by agreement submit the decision to the Federal Tribunal as court of first and last resort, provided (1) the amount involved equals at least 10,000 francs, (2) one of the parties is a domiciliary or citizen of Switzerland and (3) a Swiss court would have had jurisdiction over the case in the absence of such an agreement.[230] It is surprising that, within the area of private international relations, no attempt has apparently been made to take advantage of this extraordinary opportunity.

---

[225] See Guldener, *Int. Z.P.R.*, 71 and O. Coninx, *Die Bedeutung der Wohnsitzgarantie von Art. 59 der Bundesverfassung im internationalen Rechtsverkehr* (1942). The intracantonal repercussions of art. 59 are discussed by Fleiner and Giacometti and by Guldener, *loc. cit. supra* note 222.

[226] For details, see Guldener, *Schw. Z.P.R.*, 69, 70.

[227] *Cf.* 2 A. F. Schnitzer, *Handbuch des Internationalen Privatrechts* (4th ed. 1957-1958), 826 *ff.*; Guldener, *Int. Z.P.R.*, 169. Article 59 of the Swiss Constitution does not impede such agreements.

[228] Superior Ct. Zürich, Feb. 24, 1926, B1ZR 1926 No. 133; App. Ct. Basel, Jan. 15, 1929, SJZ 25, 284 (1929).

[229] *Bern* art. 27 (jurisdiction must be taken if at least one of the parties is domiciled or has a business establishment in the canton); *Zürich* art. 16 (if the plaintiff is domiciled in the canton). Under the laws of Basel and Geneva, the court must take jurisdiction unconditionally. The Geneva law, following French doctrine, takes a favorable approach to agreements on jurisdiction. Berthoud v. Genève Tribunal de première instance et Union des Banques Suisses, BGE 75(I) 31 (1949).

[230] Federal statute on federal civil procedure (*Bundeszivilprozess*) of December 4, 1947, art. 2, AS 1948, 485; Fleiner and Giacometti, *op. cit. supra* note 31, at 860. For a relevant intra-Swiss case, see Etat de Vaud v. Deike Stiftung, BGE 81(II) 171 (1955).

The immunity accorded by international law to foreign governments has been narrowly interpreted by Swiss courts.[231] Immunity is denied whenever the relation under dispute is one of private law and is essentially Swiss in nature.

The range of Swiss federal and cantonal jurisdiction is important in considering the administration of statutes of limitations, which in international and especially in transoceanic litigation must frequently be taken into account because of the numerous difficulties and delays connected with such litigation. According to OR article 134, the running of the statutory period, which ordinarily extends for ten years, is tolled "as long as the debt cannot be prosecuted in a Swiss court." The debtor who invokes this rule must prove that he could have been sued in Switzerland.[232]

B. *Access to Courts*

Article I, paragraph 1 of the Treaty of 1850 provides that the citizens of the two countries "shall have free access to the tribunals, and shall be at liberty to prosecute and to defend their rights before courts of justice in the same manner as native citizens." The first question is whether those citizens, being plaintiffs, are also released from the requirement to give security for costs. This point is important particularly with respect to suits brought in Switzerland because the Swiss (and other civil law) statutes demand, at variance with American law, that the security also cover the fees of the defendant's counsel, and possibly the total cost of an appellate proceeding as well.[233] The Federal Tribunal has held that the demand for security does not affect the "free access to the tribunals", and hence that the American plaintiff must provide security.[234]

However, on the basis of the treaty, the Federal Tribunal has granted the *Armenrecht* to an impecunious American who did not reside in Switzerland and who wanted to bring a suit in a lower Swiss

---

[231] E. W. Allen, *The Position of Foreign States Before National Courts* (1933), 283 (Swiss cases); *cf.* Superior Ct. of Zürich, Nov. 9, 1939, *aff'd without opinion*, Federal Tribunal, Apr. 12, 1940, B1ZR 39 No. 139 (1940).

[232] Schelling-Zollinger v. veuve Pernet, Cour de justice civile of Geneva, May 4, 1912, Semjud 1912, 463. The period of limitation may also be tolled by the inaccessibility of the court owing to war conditions. Oerlikon Machine Tool Works Buehrle & Co. v. United States, 102 F. Supp. 417 (Ct. of Claims 1952) (plaintiff a Swiss firm).

[233] *Basel* art. 44(2) (the president of the court determines at his discretion the amount of the security); *Bern* art. 70 (determination at the discretion of the court); *Geneva Proc. Civ.* art. 63 (same; security not required if the plaintiff has sufficient property in the canton); *Zürich* arts. 59, 60, 66 (determination at the discretion of the court).

[234] Instant Index Corp. v. Tribunal cantonal vaudois, BGE 60(I) 220 (1934).

court.[235] The *Armenrecht* relieves a party from the statutory costs of
the suit and may provide him with the right to have counsel appointed
by the court, without obligation to pay a fee. Moreover, the claimant
is thereby released from the obligation to give security to the defendant. There are in the American statutes corresponding provisions for
suing in forma pauperis, and they would also have to be applied in
favor of Swiss citizens living outside the United States, since the
treaty grants "reciprocal equality" for the matters dealt with in Article
I, but so far no relevant decisions have become known.

In a few states (which do not include New York, California or
Pennsylvania) preference is given to creditors residing within the
state over alien creditors, if the insolvent debtor is likewise a resident
of the state.[236] Yet to apply such a discrimination to Swiss creditors
would violate the Treaty of 1850, since that discrimination would
constitute a "burdensome condition * * * upon the enjoyment" of
their "liberty to prosecute their rights before courts of justice" — a
burdensome condition which is not imposed upon American citizens
and which, therefore, is in violation of article I, paragraph 1. While
the wording of the treaty is not very clear, this interpretation obviously concurs with its meaning.

C. *Enforcement of Foreign Judgments*[237]

Enforcement of foreign judgments is a subject closely connected
with problems of jurisdiction. Moreover, it is of primary importance
in planning the tactics of international litigation. The first point to
examine in treating the subject is whether in a given international
situation — in this case, American-Swiss — enforcement hinges on
"reciprocity" and, if so, whether reciprocity actually exists.

In Switzerland, Basel-City and Zürich deny enforcement to a foreign money judgment if the foreign state does not enforce Swiss
judgments.[238] Geneva, following French tradition, leaves the enforcement of foreign judgments to the discretion of the court, with reciprocity one of several strict requirements for enforcement.[239] Bern

---

[235] Wolfe v. Frei, BGE 76(I) 111 (1950).

[236] Disconto Gesellschaft v. Umbreit, 208 U.S. 570 (1908) concerning the law
of Wisconsin. See Nadelmann, "Foreign and Domestic Creditors in Bankruptcy
Proceedings. Remnants of Discrimination?", 91 U. Pa. L. Rev. 601, 604 (1943).

[237] R. Perret, *La Reconnaissance et l'exécution des jugements étrangers aux
Etats-Unis* (thesis Lausanne 1951); Schnitzer, *op. cit. supra* note 227, ch. 18;
T. Strehler, *Die Vollstreckung Ausländischer Zivilurteile im Kanton Zürich*
(thesis Zürich 1938); M. Petitpierre, *La Reconnaissance et l'exécution des jugements civils étrangers en Suisse* (thesis Neuchâtel 1954), 35.

[238] *Basel* art. 258; *Zürich* art. 377 (reciprocity presumed).

[239] *Geneva Proc. Civ.* art. 463.

generally enforces foreign judgments, the reciprocity prerequisite having been dropped in 1918.[240]

In 1925 the Zürich Superior Court denied enforcement to a New York judgment because the New York court lacked jurisdiction by Swiss standards and because reciprocity had not been proved from New York statutes or cases.[241] Also, according to one Swiss writer, recognition of a New York judgment was refused by the Lucerne Superior Court in 1920 on the ground of lack of reciprocity,[242] but there is no record to check this statement.

In the United States, the Supreme Court required reciprocity in *Hilton v. Guyot*.[243] In this case, however, the Court declined to enforce a French judgment on the ground that French courts review the merits of non-French judgments. Hence, a judgment rendered in a foreign state which merely requires reciprocity is not on the same plane as a French judgment. Remarkably, federal courts have declared Mexican judgments enforceable in the United States,[244] relying on a statement in *Hilton v. Guyot*, though Mexico not only required reciprocity but placed the burden of proof on the claimant.[245]

More recent developments have definitely improved the American-Swiss situation in this respect. In 1935, federal courts granted enforcement to a judgment of the Commercial Court of Bern,[246] and in 1952 to a Zürich judgment.[247] In the first case, the reciprocity requirement, which as stated above, has been renounced by Bern, was not even mentioned by the court; in the other, the burden of proof with respect to reciprocity was held to be upon the defendant. In New York State, the Court of Appeals took a strong stand as early as 1926 against the

---

[240] *Bern* arts. 396, 401. However, the cantonal government may direct the courts not to execute judgments of courts of a foreign country where reciprocity is denied.

[241] Jan. 13, 1925, B1ZR 25 No. 84 (1926). The judgment possibly purports only to decline a summary exequatur, without prejudice to an action for recognition and enforcement by way of ordinary procedure. *Cf.* Zucker, SJZ 23, 61 (1926).

[242] Petitpierre, *op. cit. supra* note 237, at 35.

[243] 159 U.S. 113 (1895).

[244] Cruz v. O'Boyle, 197 Fed. 824 (M.D. Pa. 1912); Compania Mexicana Radiodifusora Franteriza v. Spann, 41 F. Supp. 907 (N.D. Tex. 1941), *aff'd*, 131 F. 2d 609 (5th Cir. 1942).

[245] The necessity for such proof appears in the Mexican references by C. Constant, *De l'Exécution des jugements étrangers dans les divers pays* (1890), 168.

[246] Indian Refining Co. v. Valvoline Oil Co., 75 F. 2d 797 (7th Cir. 1935), on the basis of Colorado law.

[247] Gull v. Constam, 105 F. Supp. 107 (D. Colo.) likewise on the basis of Colorado law.

reciprocity requirement as formulated in *Hilton v. Guyot*,[248] and in 1953 a New York surrogate recognized a Zürich decision denying the claimant the status of a widow with respect to the estate of her alleged former husband — a declaration in rem, *i.e.*, conclusive for her status in general.[249] In both cases, however, it was emphasized that the plaintiff, having invoked the Swiss court, was bound by its decision. In California, reciprocity is not included among the express statutory prerequisites for the enforcement of foreign judgments.[250]

On the whole, there is not much danger that Swiss judgments will be denied recognition and enforcement in the United States on the ground of lack of reciprocity, or that this will happen to American judgments in Switzerland. Still, under Swiss as well as American law, recognition and enforcement of a foreign judgment may be denied on grounds other than lack of reciprocity. Thus lack of opportunity for the defendant to be heard in the foreign proceedings or incompatibility of the foreign decision with the public policy of the forum will bar the enforcement of an American judgment in Switzerland, just as they bar the enforcement of a Swiss judgment in this country. The main difference between the American and Swiss approaches lies in the fact, indicated above, that under Swiss law service of process upon the defendant does not create jurisdiction. Moreover, under article 59 of the Swiss Constitution, an American judgment against a solvent debtor domiciled in Switzerland would not be recognized there unless the defendant had voluntarily submitted to American jurisdiction.[251]

In this country, enforcement of a foreign money judgment is obtained by means of an ordinary lawsuit normally leading to a judgment embodying the foreign decision. In Switzerland the cantonal laws have developed special, and in part summary, enforcement proceedings. This is due to Switzerland's willingness to strengthen the position of foreign creditors. Summary proceedings are provided, for instance, in the cantons of Bern[252] and Zürich.[253]

---

[248] Johnston v. Compagnie Générale Transatlantique, 242 N.Y. 381, 152 N.E. 121 (1926). Shortly before the decision, the Swiss Department of Justice had predicted that New York courts would recognize and enforce Swiss judgments without probing into the reciprocity question. Burckhardt, *op. cit. supra* note 23, at §1674. The rule of the Johnston case was followed in Cowans v. Ticonderoga Pulp & Paper Co., 219 App. Div. 120, 219 N.Y. Supp. 284 (3d Dep't 1927), *aff'd*, 246 N.Y. 603, 159 N.E. 669 (1927).

[249] *In re* Zietz' Estates, 207 Misc. 22, 135 N.Y.S. 2d 573 (Surr. Ct. 1954), *aff'd*, 285 App. Div. 1147, 143 N.Y.S. 2d 602 (1st Dep't 1955), *app. denied*, 1 N.Y. 2d 748, 135 N.E. 2d 49 (1956).

[250] Cal. Code of Civil Procedure (West's Ann. Cal. Codes, vol. 21) §1915.

[251] *Supra* note 225.

[252] *Bern* arts. 396, 401 (App. Ct. competent).

[253] *Zürich* art. 377(2) (appeal to Superior Ct. of Zürich). *Cf.* Strehler, *op. cit. supra* note 237, at 24.

D. *Divorce*[254]

The international aspects of divorce are governed in Switzerland by federal legislation. Jurisdiction over divorce is vested in Swiss courts if the plaintiff is domiciled in Switzerland.[255] A foreign plaintiff has to prove (1) that his national law recognizes Swiss jurisdiction and (2) that the grounds for the divorce are admitted by Swiss law as well as by foreign law.[256] Ordinarily, an American plaintiff will not encounter difficulties on the issue of jurisdiction, which is dependent on domicile under both legal systems.[257] However, Swiss grounds for divorce are more liberal than those required by the divorce laws of some of the states, and hence the Swiss court is sometimes forced to refuse a divorce which would have been justified under Swiss law.[258]

Conversely, a Swiss citizen domiciled in the United States is not prevented by Swiss law from seeking a divorce in this country. The American divorce will be recognized in Switzerland if (1) both spouses were domiciled outside of Switzerland and (2) the American court had jurisdiction according to *American* law, an unusually liberal rule.[259] Nor would it be an obstacle to Swiss recognition should the ground for divorce be unknown to Swiss law[260] (a situation not likely to occur in American-Swiss conflict of laws). However, typical Reno or Mexican divorces of Swiss citizens will probably not be countenanced by Swiss courts.[261] It should be noted that in its administra-

---

[254] See Guldener, *Int. Z.P.R.*, 65.

[255] NAG art. 7(g) to (i); ZGB art. 144.

[256] NAG art. 7(h). The difference in grounds will be irrelevant if both are covered by the facts proved. Dame Sauthier v. Sauthier, BGE 58(II) 183, 188 (1932).

[257] The two legal systems are also akin in the determination of the wife's domicile. Under Swiss law she shares her husband's domicile unless she is entitled to separation. ZGB art. 25. On Dec. 5, 1919, the Cour de justice civile of Geneva granted a divorce to a New York wife who had a separate domicile in Geneva under both Swiss and New York law. Sicklès v. Sicklès, Semjud 42, 196 (1920).

[258] Divorces were also granted by the Zürich court of first instance in the following cases: June 10, 1914, SJZ 13, 72 (Ohio law); Oct. 7, 1930, SJZ 27, 267 (Wisconsin law); Nov. 3, 1931, SJZ 28, 250 (Massachusetts law). The parties were treated as *Angehörige* (citizens) of the state in question, in the first and third cases expressly because domiciled there. Divorce was denied by the Zürich Superior Court, June 8, 1921, BIZR 21 No. 3 (1922) (Georgia law, not in accordance with ZGB art. 142, which also runs counter to New York law). This list illustrates the prominent role of Zürich in Swiss-American private relations.

[259] ZGB arts. 137 *ff.*

[260] NAG art. 7(g), par. 3. The foreign tribunal must have jurisdiction under its own law. Spouses Fehr, BGE 80(II) 97 (1954) (Louisiana judiciary; spouses dual citizens).

[261] Swiss Dept. of Justice, Mar. 24, 1950 and Mar. 30, 1949, SchwJbIntR 6, 237, 238 (1949). In K. v. C., SchwJbIntR 13, 244 (1956), the defendant American wife had obtained a Reno divorce from her English husband and had remarried in the United States; a divorce suit of the first husband, who had

tive capacity the Federal Council has directed the registrars handling status matters to refuse registration of this kind of divorce.[262]

Instead of turning to the courts of their domiciliary state, Swiss citizens living abroad may seek divorce in the court of their home canton under Swiss law.[263] If both spouses are domiciled in the United States, the Swiss judgment will be considered invalid in this country, as has been admitted by the Swiss Department of Justice.[264]

If American recognition of a Swiss divorce is sought on the ground that the spouses had their domicile in Switzerland at the time of the divorce, the facts behind the question of domicile will be investigated and appraised by the American court independently of the Swiss court's opinion. Available cases indicate an inclination on the part of the American courts to indulge in subtle distinctions regarding the intent of a party to transform a sojourn into a domicile or a domicile into a sojourn.[265]

E. Testimony Abroad

The testimony of a witness who resides abroad and cannot or will not attend the trial may be procured with the aid of a competent foreign court. Under civil law, this is ordinarily done by letters rogatory from court to court, while American courts prefer to confer a "commission" upon an American consul, diplomatic agent or other qualified person. At the request of a party interested in a trial abroad, American courts will also hear, and if necessary subpoena, a witness present in this country.

In the United States as well as in Switzerland, such judicial assistance is a matter for state[266] and cantonal[267] courts rather than for

---

taken his domicile in Geneva, was admitted by the Geneva tribunal of first instance. A Reno divorce of *American* spouses domiciled outside Switzerland would probably be recognized in Switzerland if recognized by the state of domicile of the parties.

[262] Circular letter of September 8, 1938. Bundesblatt der Schweizerischen Eidgenossenschaft, 1938(II) 396 (referring to Mexican divorces).

[263] NAG art. 7(g). See the Fehr case, *supra* note 260, and App. Ct. Bern, Oct. 18, 1954, SJZ 51, 226 (1955) (New York domicile; New York competence to grant divorce acknowledged).

[264] Verwaltungsentscheide der Bundesbehörden 1935 Nos. 92, 93.

[265] Recognition of a Swiss divorce was granted in Robb v. Mariani, 198 Misc. 996, 100 N.Y.S. 2d 731 (Sup. Ct. 1950), and denied in Karfiol v. Karfiol, 177 App. Div. 866, 98 N.Y.S. 2d 485 (1st Dep't 1950) [with convincing dissent]. Swiss judicial recognition of a German divorce was involved in the Zietz case, *supra* note 249.

[266] For New York, see Civil Practice Act §§294, 301, 302, 309, 310-312.

Since 1948, the federal courts have been authorizd to issue letters rogatory in both criminal and civil cases, 62 Stat. 948, 28 U.S.C. §1781 (1952); F. R. Civ. P. rule 28(b); F. R. Crim. P. rule 15(a), (d), but federal legislation does not authorize compliance with foreign letters rogatory.

federal authorities, although consulates may be helpful as advisers and intermediaries. A party to a Swiss judicial proceeding may turn to the American court which has jurisdiction over the witness to take a "deposition" of his testimony.[268] Swiss consuls in the United States are also allowed to take whatever testimony may be used in Swiss litigations; and in most cases the testimony does not seem to be sworn,[269] although the consul is entitled to take an oath. In some cases a notarized affidavit, if certified by the Swiss consul, may be sufficient. It all depends on the applicable Swiss law, federal or cantonal.

The difficulties are much greater in the case of an American lawsuit. Switzerland does not accord to foreign consuls the right to take evidence,[270] even when the witness is a national of the consul's country. The American method of "commissioning" American consuls is therefore inapplicable with respect to Switzerland. However, the American court may issue a letter rogatory addressed to the Swiss court, a method repeatedly indicated by New York courts.[271] But the difficulties are considerable. The letter must also address the court in its own language, and written interrogatories in English and in the particular foreign tongue must be annexed.[272] The whole procedure of the Swiss court, moreover, is dominated by Swiss law.[273] Since Switzerland has no standing arrangements with the United States in this matter as it has with many other countries, the American

---

[267] Meyer, "Obtaining Evidence in Switzerland for Use in Foreign Courts", 3 Am. J. Comp. L. 412 (1954); H. Daum, *Zivile Rechtshilfeersuchen im schweizerischen internationalen Rechtshilfeverkehr* (thesis Zürich 1938).

[268] N. Y. Civil Practice Act §310.

[269] Swiss courts do not always require the oath from witnesses. Guldener, *Schw. Z.P.R.*, 309.

[270] Statement of the Swiss Federal Council. Burckhardt, *op. cit. supra* note 23, vol. 1 at §20(III) and vol. 4 at §1674(III).

[271] *In re* Bedford Watch Co., 18 F. Supp. 1009 (S.D.N.Y. 1937) under federal law, and, more definitely, in U.S. Neckwear Corp. v. Sinaco Co., 176 Misc. 51, 26 N.Y.S. 2d 546 (Sup. Ct. 1941) under New York law. However, in Goffin v. Esquire, Inc., 271 App. Div. 955, 67 N.Y.S. 2d 639 (1st Dep't 1947), the court issued an open commission to the American consul in Geneva to take the deposition of a witness upon the condition that the moving parties, the defendants, would defray the expenses of the plaintiff and of the latter's attorney "not exceeding $3,000, to go Switzerland". (To this, the expenses of the defendants and their attorney were to be added, of course.) Motion for reargument was denied, 272 App. Div. 57, 70 N.Y.S. 2d 135 (1947). There is no further record on the case. Obviously the decree miscarried. The case is illustrative of the whole situation. *Cf.* also *Letters Rogatory: A Symposium Before the Consular Law Society* (ed. B. Grossman 1956), 41, 53.

[272] N. Y. Civil Practice Act §309-a.

[273] *Cf.* Guldener, *Int. Z.P.R.*, 21.

court would have to turn first to the State Department, which would transfer the letter through the American Embassy or through a consulate in Switzerland to the Swiss or cantonal government, to have it in turn forwarded to the Swiss court. Once the testimony is taken, all documents must go back through the same channel. There may be further difficulties, such as costs and translations, but no case of such an American-Swiss letter rogatory is known and no discussion on the subject has been published. Obviously, the existing provisions are not practicable. Considering the growing commercial relations between the United States and Switzerland, a pertinent arrangement between the two governments would be advisable.[274]

It may be added that under a New York custom, Swiss documents signed by a Swiss official and authenticated by an American consul will only be accepted by the New York authorities if the Swiss consul certifies that the authentication was made in accordance with the laws of Switzerland and of the canton concerned.

F. *Proof of Foreign Law*[275]

Despite certain similarities in basic principles, American and Swiss practices on proof of foreign law differ widely. Generally, a party relying on foreign law must allege that law and prove it if contested. If the foreign law is not proved, Swiss and American courts alike are apt to apply the lex fori.[276] In Zürich this is prescribed by statute.[277] However, Swiss rules differ from the American insofar as the court may, and to some extent must, inquire into and apply foreign law *ex officio*. Again, the Zürich law is explicit on this point.[278] Actu-

---

[274] Swiss notaries, subject to cantonal law, are not authorized to take testimony, nor would such notarial documentation be helpful in American judicial proceedings.

[275] A general discussion of the problem has been offered by this writer in *Principles of Private International Law*, *supra* note 86, at 248 (American ed.), 235 (German ed.), and with respect to New York law in "Proof of Foreign Law in New York: A Proposed Amendment", 57 Colum. L. Rev. 348 (1957). For special analyses of Swiss law, see Guldener, *Schw. Z.P.R.*, 109 and W. Bosshard, *Die Aufgabe des Richters bei der Anwendung Ausländischen Rechts* (thesis Zürich 1929).

[276] See, *e.g.*, Wertenschlag v. Barlet, BGE 41(II) 268 (1915); Desinfecta A.G. v. Kipfer, BGE 60(II) 322 (1934).

[277] *Zürich* art. 100(2), referred to by the Federal Tribunal in Productos A.G. v. Ruckstuhl, B.G.E. 81(II) 175 (1955).

[278] *Zürich* art. 100(1) and *Basel* art. 158 authorize the courts to solicit information *ex officio* and to turn for this purpose to foreign officials and authorities. Information on foreign law is not specifically mentioned, but is obviously included. *Geneva Proc. Civ.* art. 5 requires proof of foreign law from the party invoking it; otherwise Swiss law is applied. Sydlo v. Maillart, Cour de justice civile, Semjud 57, 554 (1935). In Overseas Carbon & Coke Cy. Inc. v. Kahan, Cour de justice civile, Geneva, Feb. 4, 1957 (not published), the de-

ally, the variance between the two systems is greater than would appear from their written laws.[279] The cumbersome, overexpensive and inadequate common law requirement of proof of foreign law by sworn testimony of expert witnesses is unknown in Switzerland. Generally, foreign law is ascertained without too great an effort by cooperation of court and counsel. Official gazettes, reputable commentaries, textbooks and other pertinent literary materials may be used, regardless of whether or not they were issued "by authority". A statement by Swiss or foreign consuls on foreign law is another medium of proof, and the court may solicit such a statement.[280] In complicated cases opinions of renowned experts, which do not require formal affidavits, are submitted by the parties. In short, any serviceable means of information may be employed.

G. *Arbitration*[281]

Agreements to arbitrate present or future disputes are uniformly irrevocable under Swiss law and constitute a good defense against any suit in an ordinary law court, regardless of whether the agreement calls for arbitration in Switzerland or elsewhere.[282] In some

---

fendant alleged the invalidity under the applicable English law of an agreement and submitted as proof "large extracts of English cases", but the court dismissed the plea because the defendant had failed to submit the "English legal texts"! [I am indebted for information on this case to the Geneva lawyer, Mr. J. Guyet.]

[279] See the excellent discussion by Bosshard, *supra* note 275, at 71 ff. In 1943 the courts of New York State were given discretionary power to take judicial notice of foreign law, Civil Practice Act §344-a — *i.e.*, to follow the same plain procedure which is customary with Swiss and other civil law courts — but the courts have shown little inclination to make use of that power. The strange situation has been discussed by this writer in "Proof of Foreign Law in New York: A Proposed Amendment", *supra* note 275.

[280] An instance of such a request for proof of American law is presented by Superior Court Zürich, Nov. 12, 1920, BIZR 20 No. 177 (1921).

[281] This writer has been the editor of the *Internationales Jahrbuch für Schiedsgerichtswesen* (4 vols. 1926-1934), and has later taken a somewhat skeptical approach regarding the international usefulness of private commercial arbitration in "Treaties on Commercial Arbitration — A Test of International Private-Law Legislation", 56 Harv. L. Rev. 219 (1942), translated and supplemented in Archiv des Völkerrechts 4, 384 (1954). However, arbitration agreements between borrowers and foreign lenders seem to be increasing, especially on the part of Swiss corporations. *Cf.* Delaume, "Jurisdiction of Courts and International Loans", 6 Am. J. Comp. L. 189 (1957), especially 192, n. 9. See, further, *International Trade Arbitration. A Road to World-Wide Cooperation* (ed. M. Domke 1958) and Domke, "Enforcement of Foreign Arbitral Awards in the United States", 13 Arb. J. 91 (1958).

[282] Schnitzer, *op. cit. supra* note 227, at 745; Guldener, *Schw. Z.P.R.*, 107; Fritzsche, "Schiedsgerichte in Zivilsachen nach schweizerischem Recht", 2 *Internationales Jahrbuch für Schiedsgerichtswesen* (1928), 56.

cantons, *e.g.*, Bern [283] and Zürich,[284] the summary proceeding designed
for the enforcement of foreign judgments is available also for foreign
awards. Zürich requires that the foreign award have the force of a
judgment under the foreign law, a prerequisite which under New
York law would be satisfied only if judgment were duly entered on
the award by the New York court.[285] The utilization of the Swiss
summary proceeding is dependent on reciprocity,[286] which seems to
exist in the case of New York.[287] The cantonal prerequisites for special
proceedings, such as reciprocity, do not apply where enforcement is
sought by way of an ordinary non-summary proceeding.[288] The whole
subject is unsettled except in Basel-City, where foreign awards may
be enforced by means of an ordinary lawsuit regardless of reciprocity.[289] On the whole, the Swiss courts are definitely liberal in the
field of international commercial arbitration.[290]

Concluding Remarks

Looking back at the material discussed in this Study the reader
will receive, it is believed, the impression that American parties can
rely on the lack of prejudice of Swiss courts, just as Swiss parties can
rely on the impartiality of American courts. This is by no means a
matter of course within the world of international litigation, and it is
important far beyond the judicial field. Considering American cases,
we may add the advice that in appropriate situations the party concerned should draw the attention of his lawyer to the Treaty of 1850.

---

[283] *Bern* arts. 396, 401.

[284] *Zürich* art. 368.

[285] N. Y. Civil Practice Act §§1461, 1464.

[286] Superior Ct. of Zürich, Nov. 7, 1924, B1ZR 24 No. 181 (1925).

[287] New York law does not provide any special requirements for the enforce-
ment of foreign awards. A German award was enforced by summary judgment
in Coudenhove-Kalergi v. Dieterle, 36 N.Y.S. 2d 313 (Sup. Ct. 1942) and an
English award in Sargant v. Monroe, 268 App. Div. 123, 49 N.Y.S. 2d 546 (1st
Dep't 1944); see also Stern v. Friedman, N.Y.L.J. Feb. 21, 1945, p. 691, col. 7
(City Ct.).

[288] Swiss Federal Tribunal, Mar. 26, 1920, B1ZR 19 No. 144 (1920); 2
Internationales Jahrbuch für Schiedsgerichtswesen (1928), 344 (comment by
Rheinstein, 344 *ff.*).

[289] *Basel* art. 258.

[290] Archiv des Völkerrechts 4, 405 (1954). In the only pertinent American-
Swiss case, the District Ct. of Zürich, *aff'd* by Superior Ct., Jan. 18, 1955, and
by Cassation Ct. of Zürich, B1ZR 55, 118 (1956) [also published in SchwJbIntR
13, 304, 307 (1956)] dismissed the suit of a Swiss citizen against an American
citizen because the parties had agreed upon arbitration before a Chicago arbitral
tribunal; the court even indicted that an attachment obtained by the plaintiff
on property held by the defendant in Zürich was invalid for this very reason.

APPENDIX I

Convention of Friendship, Commerce and Extradition*

[Concluded November 25, 1850; ratifications exchanged
November 8, 1855]

The United States of America and the Swiss Confederation, equally animated by the desire to preserve and to draw more closely the bonds of friendship which so happily exist between the two Republics, as well as to augment, by all means at their disposal, the commercial intercourse of their respective citizens, have mutually resolved to conclude a general convention of friendship, reciprocal establishments, commerce, and for the surrender of fugitive criminals. For this purpose they have appointed as their Plenipotentiaries, to wit:

The President of the United States, A. Dudley Mann, Special Agent of the United States on a mission to the Swiss Confederation; and the Swiss Federal Council, Henry Druey, President of the Swiss Confederation, Director of the Political Department, and Frederick Frey-Hérosée, member of the Federal Council, Director of the Department of Commerce and of Tolls:

Who, after a communication of their respective full powers, have agreed to the following articles:

ARTICLE I

The citizens of the United States of America and the citizens of Switzerland shall be admitted and treated upon a footing of reciprocal equality in the two countries, where such admission and treatment shall not conflict with the constitutional or legal provisions, as well federal as State and cantonal, of the contracting parties. The citizens of the United States and the citizens of Switzerland, as well as the members of their families, subject to the constitutional and legal provisions aforesaid, and yielding obedience to the laws, regulations, and usages of the country wherein they reside, shall be at liberty to come, go, sojourn temporarily, domiciliate or establish themselves permanently, the former in the Cantons of the Swiss Confederation, the Swiss in the States of the American Union, to acquire, possess, and alienate therein property, (as is explained in Article V;) to manage their affairs; to exercise their profession, their

---

*This is the caption used in 2 W. M. Malloy, *Treaties, Conventions, International Acts, Protocols and Agreements Between the United States of America and other Powers* 1776-1909 (1910), 1763, from which the text is taken.

industry, and their commerce; to have establishments; to possess ware-houses; to consign their products and their merchandise, and to sell them by wholesale or retail, either by themselves or by such brokers or other agents as they may think proper; they shall have free access to the tri-bunals, and shall be at liberty to prosecute and defend their rights before courts of justice in the same manner as native citizens, either by them-selves or by such advocates, attorneys, or other agents as they may think proper to select. No pecuniary or other more burdensome condition shall be imposed upon their residence or establishment, or upon the enjoyment of the above-mentioned rights, than shall be imposed upon citizens of the country where they reside, nor any condition whatever to which the latter shall not be subject.

The foregoing privileges, however, shall not extend to the exercise of political rights, nor to a participation in the property of communities, corporations, or institutions of which the citizens of one party, established in the other, shall not have become members or co-proprietors.

ARTICLE II

The citizens of one of the two countries, residing or established in the other, shall be free from personal military service; but they shall be liable to the pecuniary or material contributions which may be required, by way of compensation, from citizens of the country where they reside, who are exempted from the said service.

No higher impost, under whatever names, shall be exacted from the citizens of one of the two countries, residing or established in the other, than shall be levied upon citizens of the country in which they reside, nor any contribution whatsoever to which the latter shall not be liable.

In case of war, or of expropriation for purposes of public utility, the citizens of one of the two countries, residing or established in the other, shall be placed upon an equal footing with the citizens of the country in which they reside with respect to indemnities for damages they may have sustained.

ARTICLE III

The citizens of one of the two Republics, residing or established in the other, who shall desire to return to their country, or who shall be sent thither by a judicial decision, by an act of police, or in conformity with the laws and regulations on morals and mendicity, shall be received at all times and under all circumstances, they, their wives, and their legiti-mate issue, in the country to which they belong, and in which they shall have preserved their rights in conformity with the laws thereof.

ARTICLE IV

In order to establish their character as citizens of the United States of America, or as citizens of Switzerland, persons belonging to the two contracting countries shall be bearers of passports, or of other papers in due form, certifying their nationality, as well as that of the members of their family, furnished or authenticated by a diplomatic or consular agent of their nation, residing in one of the two countries which they wish to inhabit.

ARTICLE V

The citizens of each one of the contracting parties shall have power to dispose of their personal property within the jurisdiction of the other, by sale, testament, donation, or in any other manner; and their heirs, whether by testament or ab intestato, or their successors, being citizens of the other party, shall succeed to the said property, or inherit it, and they may take possession thereof, either by themselves or by others acting for them; they may dispose of the same as they may think proper, paying no other charges than those to which the inhabitants of the country wherein the said property is situated shall be liable to pay in a similar case. In the absence of such heir, heirs, or other successors, the same care shall be taken by the authorities for the preservation of the property that would be taken for the preservation of the property of a native of the same country, until the lawful proprietor shall have had time to take measures for possessing himself of the same.

The foregoing provisions shall be applicable to real estate situated within the States of the American Union, or within the Cantons of the Swiss Confederation, in which foreigners shall be entitled to hold or inherit real estate.

But in case real estate situated within the territories of one of the contracting parties should fall to a citizen of the other party, who, on account of his being an alien, could not be permitted to hold such property in the State or in the Canton in which it may be situated, there shall be accorded to the said heir, or other successor, such term as the laws of State or Canton will permit to sell such property; he shall be at liberty at all times to withdraw and export the proceeds thereof without difficulty, and without paying to the Government any other charges than those which in a similar case would be paid by an inhabitant of the country in which the real estate may be situated.

ARTICLE VI

Any controversy that may arise among the claimants to the same succession, as to whom the property shall belong, shall be decided according to the laws and by the judges of the country in which the property is situated.

ARTICLE VII

The contracting parties give to each other the privilege of having, each, in the large cities and important commercial places of their respective States, Consuls and Vice-Consuls of their own appointment, who shall enjoy the same privileges and powers, in the discharge of their duties, as those of the most favored nations. But before any Consul [or Vice-Consul] shall act as such, he shall, in the ordinary form, be approved of by the Government to which he is commissioned.

In their private and business transactions, Consuls and Vice-Consuls shall be submitted to the same laws and usages as private individuals, citizens of the place in which they reside.

It is hereby understood that in case of offence against the laws by a Consul or a Vice-Consul, the Government to which he is commissioned may, according to circumstances, withdraw his exequatur, send him away from the country, or have him punished in conformity with the laws, assigning to the other Government its reasons for so doing.

The archives and papers belonging to the consulates shall be respected inviolably, and under no pretext whatever shall any magistrate, or other functionary, visit, seize, or in any way interfere with them.

[Articles VIII through XVII rescinded]

ARTICLE XVIII

The present convention is concluded for the period of ten years, counting from the day of the exchange of the ratifications, and if, one year after the expiration of that period, neither of the contracting parties shall have announced, by an official notification, its intention to the other to arrest the operations of said convention, it shall continue binding for twelve months longer, and so on, from year to year, until the expiration of the twelve months which will follow a similar declaration, whatever the time at which it may take place.

ARTICLE XIX

This convention shall be submitted, on both sides, to the approval and ratification of the respective competent authorities of each of the contracting parties, and the ratifications shall be exchanged at the city of Washington as soon as circumstances shall admit.

In faith whereof, the respective Plenipotentaries have signed the above articles, under reserve of the above-mentioned ratifications, both in the English and French languages, and they have thereunto affixed their seals.

Done in quadruplicate, at the city of Berne, this twenty-fifth day of November, in the year of our Lord one thousand eight hundred and fifty.

(SEAL)   A. Dudley Mann.
(SEAL)   H. Druey.
(SEAL)   F. Frey-Hérosée.

APPENDIX II

Convention Between the United States of America and the Swiss Confederation for the Avoidance of Double Taxation with Respect to Taxes on Income

[Signed at Washington, May 24, 1951; entered into force September 27, 1951]

The President of the United States of America and The Swiss Federal Council, desiring to conclude a convention for the avoidance of double taxation with respect to taxes on income, have appointed for that purpose as their respective Plenipotentiaries:
The President of the United States of America:
Dean Acheson, Secretary of State of the United States of America, and
The Swiss Federal Council:
Charles Bruggmann, Envoy Extraordinary and Minister Plenipotentiary of the Swiss Confederation,
who, having communciated to one another their full powers, found in good and due form, have agreed as follows:

ARTICLE I

(1) The taxes referred to in this Convention are:
   (a) In the case of the United States of America: The Federal income taxes, including surtaxes and excess profits taxes.
   (b) In the case of The Swiss Confederation: The federal cantonal and communal taxes on income (total income, earned income, income from property, industrial and commercial profits, etc.).
(2) The present Convention shall also apply to any other income or profits tax of a substantially similar character imposed by either contracting State subsequently to the date of signature of the present Convention.

ARTICLE II

(1) As used in this Convention:
   (a) The term "United States" means the United States of America, and when used in a geographical sense means the States, the Territories of Alaska and Hawaii, and the District of Columbia.
   (b) The term "Switzerland" means The Swiss Confederation.
   (c) The term "permanent establishment" means a branch, office, factory, workshop, warehouse or other fixed place of business, but does not include the casual and temporary use of merely storage facilities, nor

does it include an agency unless the agent has and habitually exercises a general authority to negotiate and conclude contracts on behalf of an enterprise or has a stock of merchandise from which he regularly fills orders on its behalf. An enterprise of one of the contracting States shall not be deemed to have a permanent establishment in the other State merely because it carried on business dealings in such other State through a commission agent, broker or custodian or other independent agent acting in the ordinary course of his business as such. The fact that an enterprise of one of the contracting States maintains in the other State a fixed place of business exclusively for the purchase of goods or merchandise shall not itself constitute such fixed place of business a permanent establishment of such enterprise. The fact that a corporation of one contracting State has a subsidiary corporation which is a corporation of the other State or which is engaged in trade or business in the other State shall not of itself constitute that subsidiary corporation a permanent establishment of its parent corporation. The maintenance within the territory of one of the contracting States by an enterprise of the other contracting State of a warehouse for convenience of delivery and not for purposes of display shall not of itself constitute a permanent establishment within that territory even though offers of purchase have been obtained by an agent of the enterprise in that territory and transmitted by him to the enterprise for acceptance.

(d) The term "enterprise of one of the contracting States" means, as the case may be, "United States enterprise" or "Swiss enterprise."

(e) The term "United States enterprise" means an industrial or commercial enterprise or undertaking carried on in the United States by a resident (including an individual, fiduciary and partnership) of the United States or by a United States corporation or other entity; the term "United States corporation or other entity" means a corporation or other entity created or organized under the law of the United States or of any State or Territory of the United States.

(f) The term "Swiss enterprise" means an industrial or commercial enterprise or undertaking carried on in Switzerland by an individual resident in Switzerland or by a Swiss corporation or other entity; the term "Swiss corporation or other entity" means a corporation or institution or foundation having juridical personality, or a partnership (association "en nom collectif" or "en commandite"), or other association without juridical personality, created or organized under Swiss laws.

(g) The term "competent authorities" means, in the case of the United States, the Commissioner of Internal Revenue as authorized by the Secretary of the Treasury; and in the case of Switzerland, the Director of the Federal Tax Administration as authorized by the Federal Department of Finances and Customs.

(h) The term "industrial or commercial profits" includes manufacturing, mercantile, mining, financial and insurance profits, but does not include income in the form of dividends, interest, rents or royalties, or remuneration for personal services: Provided, however, that such excepted items of income shall, subject to the provisions of this Convention, be taxed separately or together with industrial or commercial profits in accordance with the laws of the contracting States.

(2) In the application of the provisions of the present Convention by one of the contracting States any term not otherwise defined shall, unless the context otherwise requires, have the meaning which such term has under its own tax laws.

ARTICLE III

(1) (a) A Swiss enterprise shall not be subject to taxation by the United States in respect of its industrial and commercial profits unless it is engaged in trade or business in the United States through a permanent establishment situated therein. If it is so engaged the United States may impose its tax upon the entire income of such enterprise from sources within the United States.

(b) A United States enterprise shall not be subject to taxation by Switzerland in respect of its industrial and commercial profits except as to such profits allocable to its permanent establishment situated in Switzerland.

(2) No account shall be taken in determining the tax in one of the contracting States of the mere purchase of merchandise therein by an enterprise of the other State.

(3) Where an enterprise of one of the contracting States is engaged in trade or business in the territory of the other contracting State through a permanent establishment situated therein, there shall be attributed to such permanent establishment the industrial or commercial profits which it might be expected to derive if it were an independent enterprise engaged in the same or similar activities under the same or similar conditions and dealing at arm's length with the enterprise of which it is a permanent establishment.

(4) In the determination of the industrial or commercial profits of the permanent establishment there shall be allowed as deductions all expenses which are reasonably applicable to the permanent establishment, including executive and general administrative expenses so applicable.

(5) The competent authorities of the two contracting States may lay down rules by agreement for the apportionment of industrial and commercial profits.

ARTICLE IV

Where an enterprise of one of the contracting States, by reason of its participation in the management or the financial structure of an enterprise of the other contracting State, makes with or imposes on the latter, in their commercial or financial relations, conditions different from those which would be made with an independent enterprise, any profits which would normally have accrued to one of the enterprises, but by reason of those conditions have not so accrued, may be included in the profits of that enterprise and taxed accordingly.

ARTICLE V

Income which an enterprise of one of the contracting States derives from the operation of ships or aircraft registered in that State shall be taxable only in the State in which such ships or aircraft are registered.

ARTICLE VI

(1) The rate of tax imposed by one of the contracting States upon dividends derived from sources within such State by a resident or corporation or other entity of the other contracting State not having a permanent establishment in the former State shall not exceed 15 percent: Provided, however, that this paragraph shall have no application to Swiss tax in the case of dividends derived from Switzerland by a Swiss citizen (who is not also a citizen of the United States) resident in the United States.

(2) It is agreed, however, that such rate of tax shall not exceed five percent if the shareholder is a corporation controlling, directly or indirectly, at least 95 percent of the entire voting power in the corporation paying the dividend, and if not more than 25 percent of the gross income of such paying corporation is derived from interest and dividends, other than interest and dividends received from its own subsidiary corporations. Such reduction of the rate to five precent shall not apply if the relationship of the two corporations has been arranged or is maintained primarily with the intention of securing such reduced rate.

(3) Switzerland may collect its tax without regard to paragraphs (1) and (2) of this Article but will make refund of the tax so collected in excess of the tax computed at the reduced rates provided in such paragraphs.

ARTICLE VII

(1) The rate of tax imposed by one of the contracting States on interest on bonds, securities, notes, debentures or on any other form of indebtedness (including mortgages or bonds secured by real property) derived from sources within such contracting State by a resident or corporation or other entity of the other contracting State not having a permanent establishment in the former State shall not exceed five percent: Provided, however, that this paragraph shall have no application to Swiss tax in the case of interest derived from Switzerland by a Swiss citizen (who is not also a citizen of the United States) resident in the United States.

(2) Switzerland may collect its tax without regard to paragraph (1) of this Article but will make refund of the tax so collected in excess of the tax computed at the reduced rate provided in such paragraph.

ARTICLE VIII

Royalties and other amounts derived, as consideration for the right to use copyrights, artistic and scientific works, patents, designs, plans, secret processes and formulae, trade-marks, and other like property and rights (including rentals and like payments in respect to motion picture films or for the use of industrial, commercial or scientific equipment), from sources within one of the contracting States by a resident or corporation or other entity of the other contracting State not having a permanent establishment in the former State shall be exempt from taxation in such former State.

ARTICLE IX

(1) Income from real property (including gains derived from the sale or exchange of such property but not including interest from mortgages or bonds secured by real property) and royalties in respect of the operation of mines, quarries, or other natural resources, shall be taxable only in the contracting State in which such property, mines, quarries, or other natural resources are situated.

(2) A resident or corporation or other entity of one of the contracting States deriving any such income from such property within the other contracting State may, for any taxable year, elect to be subject to the tax of such other contracting State, on a net basis, as if such resident or corporation or entity were engaged in trade or business within such other contracting State through a permanent establishment therein during such taxable year.

ARTICLE X

(1) An individual resident of Switzerland shall be exempt from United States tax upon compensation for labor or personal services performed in the United States (including the practice of the liberal professions and rendition of services as director) if he is temporarily present in the United States for a period or periods not exceeding a total of 183 days during the taxable year and either of the following conditions is met:

(a) his compensation is received for such labor or personal services performed as an employee of, or under contract with, a resident or corporation or other entity of Switzerland, or

(b) his compensation received for such labor or personal services does not exceed $10,000.

(2) The provisions of paragraph (1) of this Article shall apply *mutatis mutandis*, to an individual resident of the United States with respect to compensation for such labor or personal services performed in Switzerland.

(3) The provisions of this Article shall have no application to the income to which Article XI (1) relates.

(4)° The provisions of paragraph (1) (a) of this Article shall not apply to the compensation, profits, emoluments or other remuneration of public entertainers such as stage, motion picture or radio artists, musicians and athletes.

ARTICLE XI

(1) (a) Wages, salaries and similar compensation, and pensions paid by the United States or by the political subdivisions or territories thereof

---

°Reservation by the United States, accepted by Switzerland: "The Government of the United States of America does not accept paragraph (4) of Article X of the Convention, relating to the profits or remuneration of public entertainers."

to an individual (other than a Swiss citizen who is not also a citizen of the United States) shall be exempt from Swiss tax.

(b) Wages, salaries and similar compensation and pensions paid by Switzerland or by any agency or instrumentality thereof or by any political subdivisions or other public authorities thereof to an individual (other than a United States citizen who is not also a citizen of Switzerland) shall be exempt from United States tax.

(2) Private pensions and life annuities derived from within one of the contracting States and paid to individuals residing in the other contracting State shall be exempt from taxation in the former State.

(3) The term "pensions", as used in this Article, means periodic payments made in consideration for services rendered or by way of compensation for injuries received.

(4) The term "life annuities" as used in this Article, means a stated sum payable periodically at stated times during life, or during a specified number of years, under an obligation to make the payments in return for adequate and full consideration in money or money's worth.

ARTICLE XII

A professor or teacher, a resident of one of the contracting States, who temporarily visits the other contracting State for the purpose of teaching for a period not exceeding two years at a university, college, school or other educational institution in the other contracting State, shall be exempted in such other contracting State from tax on his remuneration for such teaching for such period.

ARTICLE XIII

A sudent or apprentice, a resident of one of the contracting States, who temporarily visits the other contracting State exclusively for the purpose of study or for acquiring business or technical experience shall not be taxable in the latter State in respect of remittances received by him from abroad for the purposes of his maintenance or studies.

ARTICLE XIV

(1) Dividends and interest paid by a corporation other than a United States domestic corporation shall be exempt from United State tax where the recipient is a nonresident alien as to the United States resident in Switzerland or a Swiss corporation, not having a permanent establishment in the United States.

(2) Dividends and interest paid by a corporation other than a Swiss corporation shall be exempt from Swiss tax where the recipient is a resident or corporation of the United States, not having a permanent establishment in Switzerland.

ARTICLE XV

(1) It is agreed that double taxation shall be avoided in the following manner:

(a) The United States in determining its taxes specified in Article I of this Convention in the case of its citizens, residents or corporations may, regardless of any other provision of this Convention, include in the basis upon which such taxes are imposed all items of income taxable under the revenue laws of the United States as if this Convention had not come into effect. The United States shall, however, subject to the provisions of section 131, Internal Revenue Code, as in effect on the date of the entry into force of this Convention, deduct from its taxes the amount of Swiss taxes specified in Article I of this Convention. It is agreed that by virtue of the provisions of subparagraph (b) of this paragraph, Switzerland satisfies the similar credit requirement set forth in section 131 (a) (3), Internal Revenue Code.*

(b) Switzerland, in determining its taxes specified in Article I of this Convention in the case of its residents, corporations or other entities, shall exclude from the basis upon which such taxes are imposed such items of income as are dealt with in this Convention, derived from the United States and not exempt from, and not entitled to the reduced rate of, United States tax under this Convention; but in the case of a citizen of the United States resident in Switzerland there shall be excluded all items of income derived from the United States. Switzerland, however, reserves the right to take into account in the determination of the rate of its taxes also the income excluded as provided in this paragraph.

(2) The provisions of this Article shall not be construed to deny the exemptions from United States tax or Swiss tax, as the case may be, granted by Article XI (1) of this Convention.

ARTICLE XVI

(1) The competent authorities of the contracting States shall exchange such information (being information available under the respective taxation laws of the contracting States) as is necessary for carrying out the provisions of the present Convention or for the prevention of fraud or the like in relation to the taxes which are the subject of the present Convention. Any information so exchanged shall be treated as secret and shall not be disclosed to any person other than those concerned with the assessment and collection of the taxes which are the subject of the present Convention. No information shall be exchanged which would disclose any trade, business, industrial or professional secret or any trade process.

(2) Each of the contracting States may collect such taxes imposed by the other contracting State as though such taxes were the taxes of the former State as will ensure that the exemption or reduced rate of tax granted under Articles VI, VII, VIII, and XI (2) of the present Convention by such other State shall not be enjoyed by persons not entitled to such benefits.

(3) In no case shall the provisions of this Article be construed so as

---

*Now §901 (b) (3) of Internal Revenue Code of 1954, 26 U.S.C. §901 (b) (3) (Supp. V, 1958).

to impose upon either of the contracting States the obligation to carry out administrative measures at variance with the regulations and practice of either contracting State or which would be contrary to its sovereignty, security or public policy or to supply particulars which are not procurable under its own legislation or that of the State making application.

ARTICLE XVII

(1) Where a taxpayer shows proof that the action of the tax authorities of the contracting States has resulted, or will result, in double taxation contrary to the provisions of the present Convention, he shall be entitled to present the facts to the State of which he is a citizen or a resident, or, if the taxpayer is a corporation or other entity, to the State in which it is created or organized. Should the taxpayer's claim be deemed worthy of consideration, the competent authority of such State shall undertake to come to an agreement with the competent authority of the other State with a view to equitable avoidance of the double taxation in question.

(2) Should any difficulty or doubt arise as to the interpretation or application of the present Convention, or its relationship to Conventions between one of the contracting States and any other State, the competent authorities of the contracting States may settle the question by mutual agreement.

ARTICLE XVIII

(1) The provisions of this Convention shall not be construed to deny or affect in any manner the right of diplomatic and consular officers to other or additional exemptions now enjoyed or which may hereafter be granted to such officers.

(2) The provisions of the present Convention shall not be construed to restrict in any manner any exemption, deduction, credit or other allowance now or hereafter accorded by the laws of one of the contracting States in the determination of the tax imposed by such State.

(3) The citizens of one of the contracting States shall not, while resident in the other contracting State, be subjected therein to other or more burdensome taxes than are the citizens of such other contracting State residing in its territory. The term "citizens" as used in this Article includes all legal persons, partnerships and associations created or organized under the laws in force in the respective contracting States. In this Article the word "taxes" means taxes of every kind or description, whether Federal, State, cantonal, municipal or communal.

ARTICLE XIX

(1) The competent authorities of the two contracting States may prescribe regulations necessary to carry into effect the present Convention within the respective States.

(2) The competent authorities of the two contracting States may communicate with each other directly for the purpose of giving effect to the provisions of this Convention.

ARTICLE XX

(1) The present Convention shall be ratified and the instruments of ratification shall be exchanged at Berne as soon as possible. It shall have effect for the taxable years beginning on or after the first day of January of the year in which such exchange takes place: Provided, however, that if such exchange takes place on or after October 1 of such year, Article VI (except paragraph (2) thereof) and Article VII of the Convention shall have effect only for taxable years beginning on or after the first day of January of the year immediately following the year in which such exchange takes place.

(2) The present Convention shall continue effective for a period of five years beginning with the calendar year in which the exchange of the instruments of ratification takes place and indefinitely after that period, but may be terminated by either of the contracting States at the end of the five-year period or at any time thereafter, provided that at least six months' prior notice of termination has been given and, in such event, the present Convention shall cease to be effective for the taxable years beginning on or after the first day of January next following the expiration of the six-month period.

Done at Washington, in duplicate, in the English and German languages, the two texts having equal authenticity, this 24th day of May, 1951.

FOR THE PRESIDENT OF THE UNITED STATES OF AMERICA:
    DEAN ACHESON   [Seal]

FOR THE SWISS FEDERAL COUNCIL:
    CHARLES BRUGGMANN   [Seal]

APPENDIX III

Convention Between the United States of America and the Swiss Confederation for the Avoidance of Double Taxation with Respect to Taxes on Estates and Inheritances

[Signed at Washington, July 9, 1951; entered into force September 17, 1952.]

The President of the United States of America and the Swiss Federal Council, desiring to conclude a Convention for the avoidance of double taxation with respect to taxes on estates and inheritances, have appointed for that purpose as their respective Plenipotentiaries:

The President of the United States of America:

Dean Acheson, Secretary of State of the United States of America, and

The Swiss Federal Council:

Charles Bruggmann, Envoy Extraordinary and Minister Plenipotentiary of the Swiss Confederation in Washington,

who, having communicated to one another their full powers, found in good and due form, have agreed as follows:

ARTICLE I

(1) The taxes referred to in this Convention are the following taxes asserted upon death:

(a) In the case of the United States of America: The Federal estate tax, and

(b) In the case of The Swiss Confederation: Estate and inheritance taxes imposed by the cantons and any political subdivision thereof.

(2) The present Convention shall also apply to any other estate or inheritance taxes of a substantially similar character imposed by the United States or the Swiss cantons or any political subdivision thereof subsequently to the date of signature of the present Convention.

ARTICLE II

(1) As used in this Convention:

(a) The term "United States" means the United States of America, and when used in a geographical sense means the States, the Territories of Alaska and Hawaii, and the District of Columbia.

(b) The term "Switzerland" means The Swiss Confederation.

(c) The term "tax" means the Federal estate tax imposed by the United States, or the inheritance or estate taxes imposed in Switzerland, as the context requires.

(d) The term "competent authorities" means, in the case of the United States, the Commissioner of Internal Revenue as authorized by the Secretary of the Treasury; and in the case of Switzerland, the Director of the Federal Tax Administration as authorized by the Federal Department of Finances and Customs.

(2) In the application of the provisions of the present Convention by one of the contracting States any term not otherwise defined shall, unless the context otherwise requires, have the meaning which such term has under its own laws.

(3) For the purposes of the present Convention, each contracting State may determine whether the decedent was at the time of death domiciled therein or a citizen thereof.

ARTICLE III

In imposing the tax in the case of a decedent who at the time of death was not a citizen of the United States and was not domiciled therein, but who was at the time of his death a citizen of or domiciled in Switzerland, the United States shall allow a specific exemption which would be allowable under its law if the decedent had been domiciled in the United States in an amount not less than the proportion thereof which the value of the total property (both movable and immovable) subjected to its tax bears to the value of the total property (both movable and immovable) which would have been subjected to its tax if the decedent had been domiciled in the United States. If a tax is imposed in Switzerland by reason of movable property being situated within the territorial jurisdiction of the tax authority (and not by reason of the decedent's domicile therein or by reason of the decedent's Swiss citizenship) in the case of an estate of a decedent who at the time of his death was a citizen of or domiciled in the United States, the tax authority in Switzerland shall allow a specific exemption which would be allowable under its law if the decedent had been domiciled within its territorial jurisdiction in an amount not less than the proportion thereof which the value of the total property (both movable and immovable) subjected to its tax bears to the value of the total property (both movable and immovable) which would have been subjected to its tax if the decedent had been domiciled within its territorial jurisdiction.

ARTICLE IV

(1) If the tax authority in the United States determines that the decedent was a citizen of or domiciled in the United States at the time of his death, and the tax authority in Switzerland determines that the deceden was a citizen of or domiciled in Switzerland at the time of his death, the tax authority in each contracting State shall allow against its tax (computed without application of this Article) a credit for the tax imposed in the other contracting State with respect to the following property included for tax by both States (but the amount of the credit

shall not exceed the portion of the tax imposed in the crediting State which is attributable to such property):

(a) Shares or stock in a corporation (including shares or stock held by a nominee where the beneficial ownership is evidenced by scrip certificates or otherwise) created or organized under the laws of such other contracting State or a political subdivision thereof,

(b) Debts (including bonds, promissory notes, bills of exchange, and insurance) if the debtor resides in such other State, or if the debtor is a corporation created or organized under the laws of such other State or a political subdivision thereof,

(c) Corporeal movable property (including bank or currency notes and other forms of currency recognized as legal tender in the place of issue) physically located in such other State at the time of death of the decedent, and

(d) Any other property which the competent authorities of both contracting States agree upon as constituting property situated in such other State.

(2) For the purpose of this Article, the amount of the tax of each contracting State attributable to any particular property shall be ascertained after taking into account any applicable diminution or credit as provided by its law other than any credit authorized by this Article.

(3) The credit provided by this Article shall be allowed only upon condition that the tax for which credit may be authorized has been fully paid; and the competent authority of the contracting State in which such tax is imposed shall certify to the competent authority of the contracting State in which credit may be allowed such information pertaining thereto as is necessary to carry out the provisions of this Article.

ARTICLE V

(1) Any claim for a credit or refund or tax founded on the provisions of the present Convention shall be made within five years from the date of death of the decedent.

(2) Any refund or credit shall be made without payment of interest on the amount so refunded.

ARTICLE VI

Where the representative of the estate of a decedent or a beneficiary of such estate can show proof that the action of the tax authorities of one of the contracting States has resulted or will result in double taxation contrary to the provisions of the present Convention, such representative or beneficiary shall be entitled to present the facts to the contracting State of which the decedent was a citizen at the time of death or of which the beneficiary is a citizen, or if the decedent was not a citizen of either of the contracting States at the time of death or if the beneficiary is not a citizen of either of the contracting States, such facts may be presented to the contracting State in which the decedent was domiciled at time of death or in which the beneficiary is domiciled. The competent authority of the State to which the facts are presented shall undertake to come to an agreement with the competent auhority of the other contracting State with a view to equitable avoidance of the double taxation in question.

ARTICLE VII

(1) The competent authorities of the two contracting States may prescribe rules and regulations necessary to carry into effect the present Convention within the respective States.

(2) The competent authorities of the two contracting States may communicate with each other directly for the purpose of giving effect to the provisions of this Convention. Any information so received shall be treated as secret and shall not be disclosed to any persons other than those concorned with the assessment and collection of taxes which are the subject of the present Convention.

(3) Should any difficulty or doubt arise as to the interpretation or application of the present Convention or its relationship to conventions between one of the contracting States and any other State, the competent authorities of the contracting States may settle the question by mutual agreement.

ARTICLE VIII

(1) The present Convention shall be ratified and the instruments of ratification shall be exchanged at Berne as soon as possible.

(2) The present Convention shall become effective on the day of the exchange of instruments of ratification and shall be applicable to estates or inheritances in the case of persons who die on or after that date. It shall continue effective for a period of five years beginning with that date and indefinitely after that period, but may be terminated by either of the contracting States at the end of that five-year period or at any time thereafter, provided that at least six months' prior notice of termination has been given, the termination to become effective with respect to estates or inheritances in the cases of person who die on or after the first day of January following the expiration of the six-month period.

DONE at Washintgon, in duplicate, in the English and German languages, . the two texts having equal authenticity, this 9th day of July, 1951.

FOR THE PRESIDENT OF THE UNITED STATES OF AMERICA:
[SEAL]   DEAN ACHESON

FOR THE SWISS FEDERAL COUNCIL:
[SEAL]   CHARLES BRUGGMANN

APPENDIX IV

Translated Articles from the NAG*

FIRST TITLE

Private Law Relations of Swiss Residents and
Sojourners in Switzerland

B. Legal Relations of Persons and Families
1. Civil capacity

Art. 7b. Foreigners who lack civil capacity and who perform juridical acts in Switzerland cannot invoke their incapicity if under Swiss law they had such capacity at the time of the act.

This provision does not apply to acts regarding family and inheritance law, or acts disposing of immovables situated abroad.

Art. 7c. The validity of a marriage celebrated between two persons one or both of whom are foreigners is governed as to each one by his national law.

The form of a marriage celebrated in Switzerland must conform with Swiss law.

Art. 7d. Every Swiss citizen domiciled abroad°° may enter into a marriage in Switzerland.

He must have the banns published by the Registry Office of his home.°°°

Art. 7e. If a foreigner domiciled in Switzerland wishes to marry there, he must have the banns published by the Registry Office of his domicile after obtaining approval of the marriage from the government of the canton of his domicile.

The approval must not be denied whenever the home State declares that it will recognize the marriage of its national with all its consequences; yet the approval may be granted even without such a declaration.

The marriage of a foreigner not domiciled in Switzerland may be

---

* Federal Law of June 25, 1891 regarding the private law relations of residents and sojourners, as amended by Civil Code of Dec. 10, 1907, Final Title, art. 59.

°° ZGB, art. 23. The domicile of every person is at the place where he resides with the intention of establishing himself there.

No one may have several domiciles at the same time.

This last provision does not apply to an industrial or commercial establishment.

Art. 24. Every person keeps his domicile until he has acquired a new one.

The place where he resides is considered to be his domicile when the existence of a prior domicile cannot be established or when he has abandoned his domicile abroad and has not acquired a new one in Switzerland.

°°° The "home" of a Swiss citizen depends on his citizenship status. ZGB art. 22(1).

celebrated with the approval of the government of the canton where it is to take place, provided it has been shown by a statement of the home State or in some other way that the marriage, together with all its consequences, will be recognized in that State.

Art. 7f. The validity of a marriage celebrated abroad in conformity with the laws there in force will be recognized in Switzerland unless the parties entered into it abroad with the obvious intention of evading the grounds of invalidity prescribed by Swiss law.

A marriage performed in a foreign country and invalid under the law of the place of marriage may be declared invalid in Switzerland only if it is also invalid under Swiss law.

Art. 7g. A Swiss spouse living abroad may bring an action for divorce before the judge of his home.

The divorce in this case is governed exclusively by Swiss law.

If the divorce of Swiss spouses living abroad has been granted by a judge competent under the law of their domicile, it will be recognized in Switzerland even if it does not conform to the requirements of the federal legislation.

Art. 7h. A foreign spouse living in Switzerland may bring an action for divorce before the judge of his domicile if he proves that under the statutes or judicial practice of his home country the ground for divorce relied upon is admittted and Swiss jurisdiction is recognized.

A ground for divorce which arose while the spouses were subject to a law different from their present law can be relied upon only if it was also a ground for divorce under the law to which they were then subject.

If these conditions are met, the divorce of the foreign spouses is in other respects governed by Swiss law.

C. Inheritance Law

Art. 22. Inheritance is governed by the law of the decedent's last domicile.

However, by testament or inheritance contract the inheritance may be subjected to the law of one's home canton.

Art. 24. Testamentary dispositions, inheritance contracts and donations in contemplation of death are valid as to form if they are in accord with the law either of the place where the disposition was made, or that of the domiciliary canton at the time of the disposition, or with the law of the last domicile or that of the home canton of the decedent.

SECOND TITLE:
Private Law Relations of Swiss Persons Abroad

Art. 28. Unless international treaties contain different provisions, the following rules apply to Swiss persons domiciled abroad with regard to personal law, family law and inheritance law:

1° Even where, according to the foreign legislation, these Swiss persons are subject to foreign law, their immovables situated in Switzerland are governed not by the foreign law but by that of their home canton instead; the home canton also exercises jurisdiction in this case.

2° Where, according to the foreign legislation, these Swiss citizens are not subject to foreign law, they are subject both to the law and the jurisdiction of the home canton.

THIRD TITLE:

Private Law Relations of Foreigners in Switzerland

Art. 32. The provisions of this statute apply by analogy to foreigners who are domiciled in Switzerland.

TABLE OF AMERICAN CASES

TABLE OF SWISS CASES

(References are to Footnotes)

Index

Index

BILATERAL STUDIES
IN PRIVATE INTERNATIONAL LAW

No. 1: American-Swiss Private International Law, New York, 1st edition 1951, 2d edition 1958,
by Arthur Nussbaum

No. 2: American-French Private International Law, New York, 1953,
by Georges R. Delaume

No. 3: American-Dutch Private International Law, New York, 1955,
by R. D. Kollewijn

No. 4: American-German Private International Law [American-German Private Law Relations Cases 1945-1955], New York, 1956,
by Martin Domke

No. 5: American-Colombian Private International Law, New York, 1956,
by Phanor J. Eder

No. 6: American-Greek Private International Law, New York, 1957,
by Albert A. Ehrenzweig, Charalambos Fragistas
and Athanassios Yiannopoulos

No. 7: American-Danish Private International Law, New York, 1957,
by Allan Philip

No. 8: American-Australian Private International Law, New York, 1957,
by Zelman Cowen

The publishers will be happy to place your name on standing order for future publications.